MANAGING STRATEGIC ACTION
Mobilizing Change

Teaching Notes

Cynthia Hardy

SAGE Publications
London • Thousand Oaks • New Delhi

SAGE Publications Ltd
6 Bonhill Street
London EC2A 4PU

SAGE Publications Inc
2455 Teller Road
Thousand Oaks, California 91320

SAGE Publications India Pvt Ltd
32, M-Block Market
Greater Kailash — 1
New Delhi 110 048

**Printed in Great Britain by Butler & Tanner
Ltd, Frome and London**

Contents

INTRODUCTION

The aim of *Managing Strategic Action* is to address the issue of strategic action: the process of strategic change, the power needed to realize strategy, and key strategic predicaments that managers often face. It provides readers with a framework that helps them to understand strategic change and to develop ways of managing it. In so doing, it counters the focus on the rational approach to strategy making, which continues to dominate much of the prescriptive literature. Instead, it emphasizes political factors that characterize strategic change which, by definition, tends to be large-scale and contentious.

The book emphasizes an action-oriented approach to learning. Rather than describe how someone else has handled a strategic change, the cases in the book set the scene and readers are invited to engage in the strategic thought process and adopt a managerial role in order to identify how they would tackle the issues involved. The 'answer' is not embedded in the case, waiting for the reader to sift through the material and uncover it. Instead, the reader must engage actively in the learning process, use his or her imagination and insight, and come up with some feasible ideas. In my experience, students find this approach particularly rewarding, especially when they prepare and present action plans in the classroom, which can then be compared and debated.

The key, then, to the successful use of the cases in the book lies in the work done by students to prepare action plans. I recommend that instructors divide the class into small groups and require each group to prepare an action plan which can be marked if the instructor wishes. One or two groups can be picked (at random) to present their ideas to the class. This process has the advantage of engaging the students actively in the material: as they prepare their particular plan and debate its merits among themselves, they develop ownership of their particular ideas and solutions. Since all the groups do this, when it comes time to defend their ideas, students will find themselves explaining, justifying and modifying those ideas in the face of a class of extremely interested spectators.

This approach has a number of pedagogical benefits. First, it significantly increases the motivation to prepare for, participate in, and learn from the classroom discussion. Second, it transforms a one-way pattern, whereby the instructor imparts his or her 'wisdom' to a class, into a multiple-way process whereby many different ideas are debated. The resulting diversity of ideas (sensible and, sometimes, not so sensible) adds considerable depth to the discussion. Indeed, I have found that by using this technique with students with work experience, I have learned as much as they did; and even inexperienced undergraduate students can be extremely inventive and creative when given rein to do so. In this way, teaching becomes a far more rewarding process for the student and the instructor alike.

The teaching notes provide updates and/or B cases (and sometimes C and D cases). Instructors may choose to copy and distribute the updates and B cases to students for discussion, or to recount the events verbally. The updates are useful for a number of reasons. First, many updates show the students the actions taken by the actual person in the situation, which they can debate and critique. Usually, the update information is designed not so much to illustrate 'right' or 'wrong' answers but to highlight the diversity of organizational parameters that have to be addressed. Instructors will note a progression from superficial to more profound ideas during the course. At the beginning, students will focus on the obvious changes — such as structural change or a new manager — but may fail to consider how those changes will truly achieve the desired effect without supporting modifications to culture, skill requirements, evaluation systems, training, reward systems, etc. The updates are useful for pointing out what students missed. A second reason for using the updates is that the situation often changes, as does real life. The students plan a series of actions and discuss them in class; and they may make sense apart from the fact that, in the real case, something unexpected happened that changed things and required a new plan of action. Finally, the updates provide a resource that is invaluable for any instructor — information that the students don't have!

The material in *Managing Strategic Action* is sufficiently diverse and flexible to suit both theory-based and practitioner-oriented teaching approaches, and to appeal to both undergraduate and graduate students. As a result, it is appropriate for a number of different types of course: to emphasize the process of strategic change, in which case the materials can be drawn primarily from the first part; to provide a political framework for organizational change using the theory from Part II; to focus on managing strategic challenges using primarily the third part; or to custom design a course by drawing on all three parts. (See Tables 1 and 2 for a summary of themes.) Sample courses are provided which show how the cases can be combined with the readings.

Table 1 *Cases matched to strategic themes*

Case	Strategic intent	Structure & form	People & HRM	Culture	Leadership	Strategic realization
Apple (A)	x	x	x	x	x	x
Apple (B)	x	x	x	x	x	x
Mrs Fields's Cookies	x	x	x	x	x	x
Montreal Trust	x	x	x	x	x	x
Automakers		x	x	x		
ICI	x	x		x	x	x
MSP		x	x	x	x	x
Tobacco Firms	x			x		
GM/EDS	x	x	x	x	x	x
AECL			x	x		
Bicycle Components	x	x		x	x	
Conglom	x	x	x	x	x	x

Table 2 *Cases matched to political themes*

	The politics of strategy making	The dimensions of power	Critical views of power and politics
Daniel		x	
Crown Corporation		x	
MSP	x	x	x
Northville and Midville	x	x	x
Tobacco Firms	x	x	x
Apple (A) and (B)	x		
Montreal Trust	x		
Mrs Fields' Cookies		x	x
Automakers	x	x	x
ICI	x	x	
GM/EDS	x		
AECL	x		
Loblaws	x		
Conglom	x	x	x

Course 1   *Managing Strategic Change*

This course focuses on the process of strategic change and the use of power to bring about new strategies. The emphasis is on a practical, managerial approach in which students learn about the components of the change process and the typical challenges involved in realizing strategy.

1. Introduction		Hardy (chapter 1) Hambrick et al.
2. Formulating strategy	Bicycle Components	Andrews
3. Strategy and environment	Apple (A)	Daft and Weick Dess and Miller
4. Structure and form	Apple (B)	Thompson and Strickland Clegg
5. Power and strategic change	MSP	Gray and Aris Hardy (chapter 13)
6. Managing people	Montreal Trust	Fulmer Kotter
8. Managing culture	Automakers	Hassard and Sharifi Fulmer and Gilkey
9. Top-down strategic change	ICI	Bourgeois and Brodwin Sadler
10. Bottom-up strategic change	Conglom	Westley Leiba and Hardy

Course 2 *Power and Politics in Organizations*

This course adopts a theoretical approach to the study of organizational politics and combines it with material that illustrates the practical realities of change. The readings provide the theoretical foundations while the cases show how the theory translates into managerial problems.

1. Introduction		Hardy (chapter 1)
2. The politics of initiation	Daniel and the Lions' Den	Hardy (chapter 13)
3. The politics of dependency	Crown Corporation	Kotter
4. The politics of culture	Automakers	Hassard and Sharifi
5. The politics of leadership	ICI	Bourgeois and Brodwin
6. The politics of ethics	Tobacco Firms	Bird and Hardy
7. The politics of stakeholders	Northville and Midville	Westley and Vredenburg
8. The politics of empowerment	Mrs Fields	Leiba and Hardy
9. The politics of collaboration	Conglom	Westley
10. The politics of strategy	MSP	Gray and Ariss

Course 3   *Managing Strategic Contexts*

This course examines some key contexts in which strategic change occurs and which give rise to particular managerial challenges as a result of the political dynamics that are present.

1. Forming strategic intent	Mrs Fields'	Andrews Dess and Miller
2. Realizing strategic intent	Montreal Trust	Hambrick et al. Fulmer
3. Managing the entrepreneurial firm	Apple (A)	Daft and Weick Gray and Ariss
4. Managing the growing firm	Apple (B)	Thompson and Strickland
5. Managing the divisionalized firm	Conglom	Westley Brodwin and Bourgeois
6. Managing innovation	Machco	Dougherty Clegg
7. Managing M&As	GM/EDS	Fulmer and Gilkey Hasard and Sharifi
8. Managing decline	AECL	Hardy (chapter 18) Tobacco Firms
9. Managing globally	Bicycle Components	Wortzel
10. Managing sustainable development	Loblaws	Westley and Vredenburg

PART I UNDERSTANDING THE STRATEGIC CHANGE PROCESS

Introduction

This part examines various aspects of the strategic change process. The chapters by Andrews on strategy formulation, by Dess and Miller on competitive advantage, and by Thompson and Strickland on structure provide the basic grounding in strategy and structure. Instructors wishing to cover strategy formulation and implementation in the same course will find these chapters useful. Instructors wishing to focus on managing strategic change may still want to use these chapters as a link to other strategy courses.

The Daft and Weick chapter discusses the link between strategy and environment. Their model illustrates both how strategy can create an environment, as in the case of the embryonic Apple, and how 'reading' an environment may provoke a new strategy. As part of any discussion on the environment, the students can debate the role of environmental triggers — it seems that as organizations become larger and more bureaucratic, a more radical event is needed to provoke strategic change, as in the case of ICI.

While Thompson and Strickland cover basic organizational structures, the chapter by Clegg takes a look behind formal structure to show how Japanese companies have created more flexible coordinating arrangements. Fulmer provides a basic overview of human resource considerations. The different components of human resource management can be fleshed out by taking a closer look at the cases, where it should be clear to students that the appropriate selection and recruitment, training and development, performance appraisal, and reward systems are crucial if organizational members are to sustain the strategic direction. Culture is an integral part of strategic change — it can either hinder it or facilitate it. The complexity of managing culture is discussed by Hassard and Sharifi and, although it may be difficult to change the underlying organizational culture, certain manifestations of it can be modified. Leadership styles are tackled by Bourgeois and Brodwin. The tendency in much of the literature has been to emphasize the CEO as a commander or architect of strategic change. Students should be pushed to consider other change agent roles, as well as the situation where there is no identifiable agent.

The Hambrick chapter can be used equally well as either an introduction or a conclusion to the course. Its basic premise and that of all the cases in the book is that, for strategic change to be effective, all the relevant supporting organizational changes must be made. Strategic intent will only be realized if the organization is redesigned to align with it.

The cases illuminate these components of the strategic change process in various ways. The list of themes below can be used to aid course design and preparation and/or be used as questions to students.

Key themes in the strategy making process

Introduction
What is the strategic intent of the organization?
What organizational changes are needed to support the strategy?
What levers exist to shape/promote strategic change?
What are the main challenges in bringing about strategic change?
Strategic intent
What strategic intentions have been formed?
How have they been formed?
Who subscribes to them?
Is the environment enacted or created by strategy?
Is the environment a constraint on strategy?
Is the environment a stimulus to strategic change?
How does the organization 'read' the environment?
What competitive advantages does the strategy offer?
What demands does it place on the organization?
Strategic alignment
What are the main differences of the traditional structures?
What are the advantages and disadvantages of each?
What are the other ways of achieving flexibility and innovation?
What are the informal aspects of structure?
What are the systems and coordinating mechanisms?
How can human resource policies help strategy making?
How should these policies be changed?
What is the nature of the existing (sub)cultures?
What are their implications for strategy?
What cultural changes are required?
How can they be carried out?

Who is the change agent?
Is there always a change agent?
If not, how is change orchestrated?

Strategic realization
Is the organization aligned around the strategy?
What elements are misaligned?
What is the current stage of the organization?
What future problems can be anticipated?
How can they be solved?

Summary
Has strategic intent been realized?
How?
What organizational parameters were changed to facilitate it?
Do organizational parameters still need to be changed?
What changes are likely in the future?

Apple (A)

A very effective way to use both Apple cases is, near the beginning of the course, to ask students to prepare an action plan for Sculley. Because students have all heard of Apple (and some will know quite a lot about the technical aspects), they enjoy becoming engaged in the action-planning process. I find it useful to allow one group to present; invite questions from the audience, who will have quite different ideas (any recommendations that owe too much to 20/20 hindsight can be countered by asking students their views based on information available at the time); use the ideas to stimulate discussion around the pros and cons of different actions; and then summarize the key points. The summary should highlight the need for students to (a) make their strategic choice about which markets to enter, and (b) undertake a comprehensive assessment of the problems *before* they design an action plan. The former is important because implementation issues will vary according to whether Apple decides to tackle the corporate market or not (and students will hold conflicting views on this). For example, IBM compatibility may be more critical if Apple decides to tackle the corporate market than if it does not. The latter is important because the action plan needs to be checked to see if it did, indeed, solve the problems.

A useful device in summarizing is to ask the class for a recap of all the problems. They include: structure; reporting relationships between Jobs and Sculley; product development and overlap; software development; distribution; pricing; marketing; company image; cost cutting; IBM compatibility; hiring new personnel; culture and morale. Many of these issues are interconnected and depend on the initial strategic choice of which markets segments to enter. Students can then be asked whether their action plans addressed any or all of these problems. Typically, students completely gloss over the issue of structure, particularly if the case is used early on in the course, or advocate unnecessarily complex structures (such as a matrix or adhocracy). A discussion of how organizational structure should support strategic choice can be entered into here. Another common shortcoming of student recommendations concerns the lack of concrete detail — the summary can be used to push students into saying exactly how employees should be rewarded, how product development can be stimulated, which products should be cut, etc. Finally, debates over such matters as whether to go into the business market, whether to develop software in-house, whether to build a direct sales force, will arise. Apart from the obviously infeasible ideas, instructors can use these debates to raise the pros and cons of the various actions and draw attention to the fact that while there may be visibly 'wrong' ways of implementing a strategy, there is rarely a self-evident 'right' way of doing things.

Instructors may, then, like to discuss what Sculley did, in fact, do either by recounting events or handing out the following update.

Apple (A): Update

In mid-September 1983, Sculley reduced the Lisa's price by 18 per cent and 'unbundled' it, allowing the hardware and software to be sold separately, which was a drastic revision of Apple's marketing strategy. He also started to develop a strategy to counter IBM. The mainstay of the new strategy was the Macintosh — a less powerful, lower priced member of the Lisa family. It would be capable of word processing, drawing and financial spreadsheets. The Lisa II — a cheaper, faster model than the original — was also planned. It would be capable of using the Mac's software (though the Mac was not powerful enough to run Lisa software). A portable version of the Apple IIe was also announced. These three products (the Apple IIe, the Lisa and the Macintosh) were to be the basis of a 'technology-driven' and 'product-oriented' strategy (Sculley, quoted in *Business Week*, 16 January 1984: 79). Apple continued to target the small business, application-specific, and educational markets, and to promote Apple as an *alternative* to IBM.

> We're not going to sell five million computers a year by being IBM compatible. We're going to do it by making a second industry standard. (Jobs, quoted in *Fortune*, 20 February 1984: 98)

The Mac symbolized Jobs' vision of Apple as a unique and different product. It went against conventional wisdom — and the company had originally become successful by going against the conventional wisdom.

The second part of Sculley's strategy was the rationalization of product lines into two product divisions (Figure I). Apple II and Apple III products were combined in the Apple II division, headed by Del Yocam, a six-year veteran of Apple who had come up through the manufacturing ranks. The Lisa and Macintosh became the responsibility of the Mac division, and Jobs was named its Vice-president. The aim of the two new divisions with decentralized manufacturing, product development and marketing functions was to facilitate a coherent product strategy, since the Apple III, Lisa and Mac each used different operating systems and the Mac was not compatible with any of its predecessors. These difficulties had been partially attributed to the fact that Jobs had earlier stormed off the Lisa development team, complaining that a low-cost, easy to use product was needed for the masses, rather than a high-priced, business-oriented product. While he had helped develop the far more successful Macintosh, Jobs' actions had inhibited the development of a coherent product line.

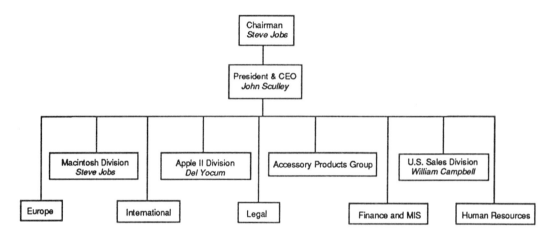

Figure 1 *Apple organization chart (circa 1984)*

Source: Adapted from *Transnational Management, Text, Cases and Readings in Cross-Border Management* by Christopher A. Bartlett and Sumantra Ghosal, Irwin Publications, Homewood, Illinois, 1992: 726

Sculley also attempted to control costs, reduce overhead, and rationalize product lines. He centralized reporting relationships, and 15 general managers who had previously reported to group vice-presidents now reported directly to him. Almost half of the 15 member senior management team was replaced or left. The workforce of 5,300 was reduced to 4,600 between July 1983 and January 1984. Hiring slowed from 250 to 50 a month. The generous profit sharing programme was suspended. He introduced marketing techniques and disciplines, and tried to raise awareness inside the company of the competitive environment it faced. 'He made us respect IBM' (*Fortune*, 9 July 1984: 181). More money was pumped into marketing and advertising as the marketing budget jumped to $80 million from $12 million in two years, while the research budget remained stable.

Despite their personality differences, the intense, level-headed Sculley and mercurial, tempestuous Jobs managed to forge a strong friendship. It had started during the 'courtship' period when Jobs had persuaded Sculley to join Apple, and continued despite the fact that Jobs was both above (as Chairman with a 12 per cent ownership stake) and below (as Vice-president of the Mac Division) Sculley. Both men had high praise for the other one and, although they often had different views, they met several times a day to reach agreement.

> Steve and Sculley have the same goals but they reach them in different ways. Like new-product development: Sculley wants a new product because he wants to diversify the product line; Steve wants it because it's just the best idea he's ever seen and he can't wait to do it. (Employee quoted in *Fortune*, 20 February 1984: 100)

Sculley believed that he and Jobs shared the role of leader.

> I viewed my role as a coach to a brilliant young founder, someone who would help him develop the skills he was going to need maybe five or six years later. Even though I held the title of CEO, I knew it was a shared leadership title with the founder. (Sculley quoted in *Inc*, October 1987: 49)

Sculley also managed to fit into Apple's unique culture. For example, he sent out tickets to *Indiana Jones and the Temple of Doom* with employees' paycheques. He had mastered the intricacies of both hardware and software technology and, having abandoned his business suit in favour of a more casual look, was rumoured to wear a tie less often than Jobs. Employees seemed to be happy with his management style and the changes he had made.

Question

- Do you think Sculley has solved Apple's problems?

Source Material

Dreyfus, J., 'John Sculley rises in the West', *Fortune*, 181-4, 9 July 1984.
Fortune, 'Apple changes strategy', p. 75, 17 October 1983.
Kessler, K., 'Apple's pitch to the *Fortune* 500', *Fortune*, 53-6, 15 April 1985.
Morrison, A., 'Apple Bites Back', *Fortune*, 86-100, 20 February 1984.

Apple (B)

Apple (B) can be used in the class following Apple (A). The discussion can start by comparing the situation at the end of the two cases: what did John Sculley achieve during his first two years at Apple? The instructor can recap the problems identified in Apple (A) and see if they still exist in 1985: a lack of strategy for the corporate market; tension between dealers and a possible sales force; software development; product innovation; IBM compatibility; product overlap; advertising; pricing; morale; and the loss of key people. Most of these problems are still there in 1985, with the added complications of a recession in the PC market and losses for the company. Students can debate why Sculley has been unsuccessful: was it his lack of experience or Jobs' desire for control? They may also comment on the way in which Steve Jobs was handled and the political issues associated with these two protagonists and the Board.

Students can be asked to provide an action plan for Sculley at the end of Apple (B). This attempt is usually a big improvement on earlier attempts though, typically, students overlook the losses and the need to come up with a plan to reduce costs. Apple can be used to illustrate the Greiner article (listed in the Additional Reading), and the transition from an entrepreneurial to a more bureaucratic firm with the accompanying need for more controls and procedures which, in this case, is exacerbated by the losses. The update shows that Sculley did initially introduce a functional, centralized organization. Instructors should note that students tend to be seduced by Greiner's phase of collaboration, so they may need to spend some time talking to students about why it is an expensive structure to have in a recession when managers need to reduce costs and exert control.

The update brings the students to the point where Apple announced its joint venture with IBM. The class can be wrapped up by referring back to the list of problems identified earlier and seeing how many have been solved. Apple can also be used to illustrate the different forms of structure that exist and their advantages and disadvantages. While there is no detailed information on Apple's organization, charts showing the broad outlines (see Figures 1 and 2) do illustrate some of the key issues and help students gain a more grounded understanding. The 1984 chart shows the emphasis on product development that Sculley was trying to achieve, particularly as far as the Mac was concerned. The 1985 chart (Figure 1) shows a functionalized structure as Sculley attempted to cut costs and assert control. The 1987 structure (Figure 2) embodies more delegation and a focus on geographic markets, as Apple tailored its strategy to meet the needs of different countries.

Finally, an interesting way to close the session is to ask students whether Sculley ever had a strategy for Apple. Opinions will vary from those who think he had no strategy and was capable only of rationalization, to those who think he is the driving force behind Apple. Another way to wrap up Apple is to assign students to conduct a library search to find out about recent events and performance.

The picture is far from clear. In 1990, Sculley had become Chief Technologist — a decision which had aroused considerable criticism. In 1991, shares hit an all time high as the Powerbook (a lap-top computer) was a resounding success. In 1993, however, Sculley stepped down as CEO and was replaced by Spindler. With no new product in the pipeline, the stock price dropped 25 per cent, earnings remained flat and lay-offs were expected once again.

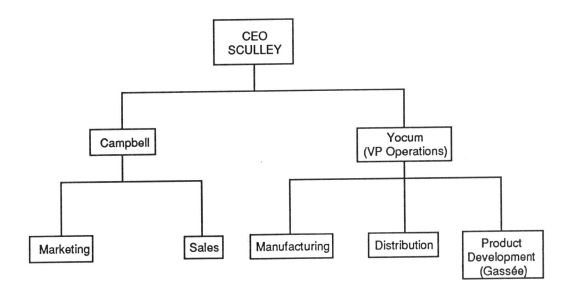

Figure 1 *Apple organization chart (circa 1985): functional structure*

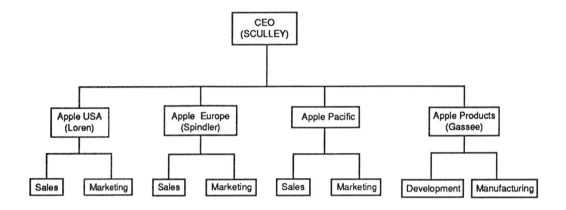

Figure 2 *Apple organization chart (circa 1987): geographic divisions*

Apple (B): Update

Sculley split Apple into two functional groups — one for product development and manufacturing and the other for marketing and sales — instead of the previously decentralized divisions. His aim was to reduce duplication and ensure a lower breakeven point. It was hoped that the merging of the product divisions would end the intense rivalry between Apple II and Mac personnel that had sapped morale and resulted in a series of defections from the company. Del Yocam was put in charge of all engineering, manufacturing and distribution operations. Gassée reported to Yocam and headed product development. William Campbell, previously marketing director of the Apple II division, was responsible for marketing and sales. Sculley laid off one-third of the 6,000 workers, including part of the field sales force that had recently been hired, and closed three of its six factories. He instituted strict financial controls, formal reporting procedures, and tough product development deadlines. As a result of these changes, Sculley was able to pare the breakeven point to quarterly sales of $325 million from $400 million. Earnings increased 23 per cent in the quarter ending December 1985, and profit margins improved to 52 per cent of sales, the highest in years. But sales fell by 23 per cent and market share continued to slip to 11 per cent (from 19 per cent two years earlier). Apple's financial health was not under any serious threat, however, since the company was sitting on $440 million in cash.

What *was* fragile, however, was the morale of the employees. Many were still loyal to Jobs and resented his departure, while others were concerned about the recent large scale layoffs and the future direction of the company. The Lisa had been discontinued in 1985 and the Mac continued to disappoint with less than one-quarter of the expected 2 million units sold. Sculley's lack of technical experience and understanding of the needs of corporate users had prevented him from realizing how off track the Mac was.   As a result, the aging Apple II family remained the company's bread-winner. An open architecture that would allow the Mac to communicate with IBM machines had still not been delivered.

In an attempt to solve these problems, Sculley relied on Jean Louis Gassée to steer product development; hired a number of engineers from companies like Hewlett Packard to boost product development expertise; and purchased a $15 million Cray 'supercomputer' to speed product development. Sculley also cut the price of the Mac by 20 per cent in an effort to improve sales. The focal point of Apple's strategy to enter the business market was desktop publishing, in which IBM did not have a competitive product. Apple planned software and a laser printer that would make the Mac capable of high-quality printing. Even so, Apple faced considerable competition: Xerox had developed a system that would tie IBM machines to their laser printers. Furthermore, Apple's reliance on dealers continued to put the company at a disadvantage when selling to large business customers. Sculley was forging alliances with companies that had direct sales forces, such as minicomputer company Prime Computer Inc. Unfortunately, Prime only sold its products to individual end users, and Apple still lacked direct access to the corporate businesspeople who made the major computer purchasing decisions.

Sculley also had to work hard to keep key people and rebuild morale in all parts of the company, not just in design and engineering. All Apple employees became eligible for bonuses, and Sculley retained aspects of the old Apple culture: there were still free popcorn and Friday beer busts, and just before Christmas 1986, employees were bussed to see *Star Trek IV*. Employees continued to leave Apple, however, because they had felt it had become the same as any other big boring company in which employees were simply a cog in the wheel.

But Sculley's efforts bore the desired results: profits doubled between 1985 and 1987 and the price of Apple stock soared more than 500 per cent. Shipments of the Mac doubled in 1986 despite an increase of only 9 per cent in world wide personal computer sales. Desktop publishing exceeded Sculley's expectations as some 50,000 systems were sold in 1986; and Microsoft's Excel enabled Apple to compete head to head with Lotus 1-2-3. Apple's 1986 earnings increased by 150 per cent to $154 million and shares were trading at over $40, a three-year high. The company had over $500 million in cash and no debt. In the Spring of 1987 two new 'open' versions of the Mac were launched that were far more adaptable than older models. They helped boost both earnings and profits further in 1987. Most of the increase came from the business market. Margins exceeded 50 per cent and were among the best in the business. In 1986 Sculley promoted Del Yocam from Vice-president (Operations) to Chief Operating Officer.

Unfortunately, the latter part of the 1980s brought a new set of issues for Sculley to address. In 1987, IBM and Microsoft introduced the OS/2 operating system to run on IBM's new PS/2 line of personal computers. The product failed to sell well but, instead of lowering Mac prices to expand market share during this period while the competition was adjusting, Sculley opted for premium pricing and high margins. He restructured the company again in 1987 — into three sales and marketing divisions covering the USA, Europe and the

Pacific, and a separate division to handle development and manufacturing. Allen Loren became President of Apple USA, and Gassée was made President of Apple Products. The two individuals were very different. Loren was a hard-nosed New York businessman, while Gassée was a flamboyant Frenchman renowned for his earring and flashy shirts. Tensions soon started to develop between these two protagonists, one of whom would be the likely successor to Sculley, especially when Del Yocam retired in 1988. New products also caused problems. The Mac Portable was introduced in 1989, but since it weighed more and cost more than competitive products, it hardly qualified as a success. The new Macs were as much as 36 per cent more expensive than comparable IBM and Compaq machines, which cut into Apple sales. The outlook did not look any brighter when, in 1990, Microsoft announced Windows 3 which gave IBM machines graphic display capabilities that rivalled those of the Mac.

Earnings fell by 30 per cent in 1989 and Apple's share of the market dropped to 9 per cent in 1990. Major cuts (salary freezes, layoffs, phasing out company cars, and modifications to the profit sharing plan) were announced to reduce spending levels. Internal problems continued to build, however, as Loren's abrasive style earned him many enemies, and his constant reorganizations of Apple USA unsettled employees. Sculley forced his resignation in 1990, which was soon followed by Gassée's departure after a curtailment of his responsibilities.

Sculley decided to appoint Michael 'Diesel' Spindler as his second-in-command. Spindler had been responsible for tripling Apple Europe's revenues over the previous three years. His appointment symbolized the transition of Apple from a counter-cultural entrepreneurial organization to a large (25,000 employees), staid company. 1991 saw the adoption of 'off-the-shelf' technology to reduce the cost and time of development (technology purchased from other firms as opposed to developed in-house); a revival of the company's focus on the educational market; and the abolition of its direct sales force to placate unhappy dealers. The 1987 decision to get out of the software business was reversed with an announcement that Apple was to buy back 20 per cent of its Claris software subsidiary and operate it as a wholly owned subsidiary. Apple also reversed its traditional refusal to license technology by signing agreements with Sony (to develop a new notebook-size Macintosh computer) and Toshiba.

On 3 July 1991, IBM and Apple announced a technology-sharing alliance. Everyone was surprised to see the age-old rivals move into an agreement requiring them to share proprietary technology and disclose future product plans. The alliance was hailed as the beginning of 'the second decade of personal computing' by IBM CEO John Akers. It included: cross-licensing of current technologies; joint development of a new operating system; and joint ventures to develop the technology and products for emerging areas such as multi-media and object programming.

> This is the decade in which Apple moves from being a wild card in the industry to playing in the mainstream. We learned in the 1980s that we can't do it alone. (Sculley, quoted in *Fortune*, 4 November 1991: 151)

Questions

- Did John Sculley have a strategy for Apple in the 1980s?
- Does he have a strategy for the 1990s?

Source Material

Business Week, 'The palace revolt at Apple Computer', p. 38, 17 June 1985.
Business Week, 'Can John Sculley clear up the mess at Apple', 70-1, 29 July 1985.
Business Week, 'Steve Jobs vs Apple: What caused the final split', p. 48, 30 September 1985.
Business Week, 'Apple, Part 2: The no-nonsense era of John Sculley', 27 January 1986.
Business Week, 'Apple's comeback', 84-9, 19 January 1987.
Business Week, 'Apple turns from revolution to evolution', 27 January 1989.
Business Week, 'Apple's woes can't just be reshuffled away', p. 32, 12 February 1990.
Business Week, 'The toughest job in the computer business', 118-22, 19 March 1990.
Business Week, 'Apple Computer', 86-96, 15 October 1990.
Fortune, 'Sculley's lessons from inside Apple', 108-20, 14 September 1987.
Fortune, 'Growing Apple anew for the business market', 36-7, 4 January 1988.
Fortune, 'John Sculley on sabbatical', 27 March 1989.
Fortune, 'Yet another strategy for Apple', 22 October, p. 22, 1990.
Inc, 'Corporate antihero: John Sculley', 49-59, October 1987.
Inc, 'Entrepreneur of the decade', 115-28, April 1989.
Perspectives, 'Is Apple in trouble?', 47-52, 5 February 1990.
Uttal, B., 'Behind the fall of Steve Jobs', *Fortune*, 5 August 1985.
Uttal, B., 'The adventures of Steve Jobs (cont'd)', *Fortune*, 119-24, 14 October 1985.

Montreal Trust

Montreal Trust can be used to touch on virtually all the aspects of organizational design (or redesign) necessary for strategic change. It can be used to pin-point all the relevant factors: people, information systems, communication, structure, products, marketing, etc. It is also a very effective assignment since students are presented with a general description of the situation and can be required to prepare a comprehensive action plan. I use it on the first day of the course and then return to it on the last day, in both cases by asking students to present an action plan. The contrast between the two 'answers' helps to demonstrate to students how their understanding of change has developed during the course. Instructors can either draw on the material in the B Case to influence the classroom discussion, or allow students to talk freely about their ideas and hand it out for comment afterwards so that students can debate or critique what Leclaire actually did.

The case can be used to illustrate a number of other key issues. First, Leclaire had to deal with a number of challenges because he was a new manager. He had to take the time to study and learn before he could take action. He had to address a lack of credibility because he came from the Systems Division and had no experience in the branch network. He also had to deal with a senior management team that was resistant to new ideas and ways of operating. The Senior Vice-president (Branch Operations) posed a particularly difficult problem. On the one hand, Leclaire needed his knowledge and expertise. On the other hand, this extremely powerful individual probably believed that the top job should have been his. Second, Leclaire modified the structure changed, not only in response to strategic demands, but also in response to *people*. The first change in structure allowed him to introduce some new faces. The second removed a powerful adversary and the third helped to encourage team work and a customer focus. The structural concerns also demonstrate the dilemma between functional and product organization. No structure is perfect — all have weaknesses and it is a matter of identifying and compensating for them. Finally, Leclaire's style is particularly appropriate to a relatively small organization with a niche strategy involving high-added value. He was able to spend the necessary time talking and listening to his regional vice-presidents and branch managers.

This situation may change in the future, however. In March 1993, it was announced that Montreal Trust would be sold to another, much larger Canadian bank. Serge Leclaire was waiting to see exactly how the new owner proposed to incorporate PSD into its banking operations. Students can consider what arguments they would use to convince this new stakeholder to allow Personal Services Division to pursue its strategy.

Montreal Trust (B)

Leclaire knew that he would have to convey his ideas clearly if employees in the branches were to act on them. He engaged in an intensive communication strategy by speaking to individuals personally, showing them figures that proved his case, and sending memos. In the case of the poor response to the call for more telemarketing he issued a memo with eye-catching graphics and a strongly worded condemnation of the lack of action. In the case of the RRSPs, he cited the example of two very successful branches to show what could be done. In both cases, he composed the memos himself to avoid watering down his vision and personality. He continued to review individual branch performance on a monthly basis to make it clear that he was serious about the new initiatives. He also considered the idea of a regular newsletter to use as a vehicle for communication to the branches. It became clear, however, that chasing after specific mistakes was not enough to bring about the new strategy. More fundamental changes were necessary to solve problems of resistance and avoid mistakes.

Leclaire knew he had to extend his direct contact with the branch network. Between September and November 1990, he commissioned and participated in 13 focus groups, each consisting of five branch managers. They were asked to identify the most serious problems or threats facing PSD and produced some 50 areas of concern, which were synthesized by Leclaire into six broad objectives. There was a clear consensus on these objectives, which embodied a more sophisticated consumer and marketing orientation: (1) define the target market and direct all promotional activities towards it; (2) introduce more new products and product enhancements; (3) increase customer awareness; (4) improve information systems; (5) improve decision making and decentralize authority; (6) address human resource issues by bringing training, career development, incentive schemes and performance measures into line with the new strategy. The objectives were then incorporated into a series of action plans and new programmes: a new RRSP telemarketing campaign; the Executive Money Master Account (a combination of savings and checking accounts and a line of credit); and product profiles — cards that kept employees up-to-date on all products.

The focus groups had a number of advantages. They helped to make branch managers aware of the problems; secured their commitment by involving them in the change process; provided Leclaire with grass-roots information; and allowed him to meet branch managers face-to-face. As his initial experiences had showed, direct communication was important: even though Leclaire simplified his messages as much as he could, they were often misunderstood. Also people were often unwilling to admit when they did not understand. Leclaire reinforced the focus groups by developing tools to help employees adjust to the new marketing orientation. He used the new database. Since customer information was incomplete, branch personnel were given the task of calling clients to check the information. It gave them the opportunity to establish relationships and identify potential openings. For example, if a client reported that he or she had a mortgage but not with Montreal Trust, the employee could inform them that special discounts were often available to customers — would they be interested if such a programme was launched? The employee could then call the client back with a special mortgage package with a high degree of confidence instead of having to rely on 'cold' calls and 'hard' sells.

Leclaire also had to develop more accountability among branch managers to reduce the number of bad loans, maintain existing clients, and emphasize more profitable products. The concept of the *cross sell ratio* was replaced by *profit per household*. Instead of pushing credit cards, it emphasized long-term client relationships involving profitable products. The concept of productivity was replaced by the idea of the *portfolio*, which measured the amount of new and lost business, both of which were factored into the branch managers' bonuses. In addition, managers were given a budget for bad loans — if it was exceeded, the losses would reduce the branch's revenues and affect the manager's bonus. Business with mortgage brokers was centralized in three locations where experts could evaluate the quality of the loans. Previously, some branch managers had been too quick to accept brokers' appraisals of property in efforts to increase their business. As a result, properties had been overvalued and loan losses had increased. Now, these problems could be avoided before any damage was done.

At the same time as working with the branches, Leclaire started to change the culture of his senior management team, which had previously been traditional and hierarchical. He wanted to create a more challenging, innovative culture. He used an external consultant to run meetings with no fixed agenda, in which all participants were encouraged to say what was on their mind. It started with the recounting of recent negative events to stimulate discussion and identify problems. The meeting would then move on to brainstorming to find solutions. For some individuals these meetings were uncomfortable — they often resulted in disagreement, took up a lot of time, and rarely produced nice, neat solutions. In many respects, however, they were highly productive since they got to the bottom of a problem and sparked subsequent actions that, in the long term, led to more enduring solutions.

The main component of the culture change at both senior and branch levels was meetings — lots of them. Leclaire estimated that he spent 60 per cent of his first year in PSD in group and individual meetings. Some were informal, unplanned one-to-one encounters, others were carefully scheduled to bring a variety of different groups together. For example, Leclaire would arrange two-day meetings with the regional vice-presidents. He would see them alone on the first day so they could freely discuss issues that related to other groups. He would then bring in his senior vice-presidents to enhance mutual understanding and create a team spirit. Leclaire also included regional vice-presidents and some branch managers in brainstorming to bring these lower levels into direct discussions with more senior managers. He wanted to develop more autonomy and accountability at lower levels so that they would learn how to become responsible for their own 'business', and to ensure that senior managers were willing to relinquish some control. These changes marked a significant departure from the old culture where regional and branch personnel did what their superiors told them.

In the middle of these cultural changes — in October 1990 — Leclaire made a major structural change. He reorganized PSD into three basic product groups: retail lending services, trust and investment services, and retail banking services (Figure 1). Each product group was headed by a Product Vice-president who reported directly to the Executive Vice-president. The Vice-president (Marketing Communications) — previously the Vice-president (Marketing) — now reported directly to the Executive Vice-president, and was responsible for determining consumers' product needs and liaising with the product vice-presidents on product development. The Planning and Control Department monitored the Division's performance. All senior personnel retained their positions, but the reorganization allowed Leclaire to promote two new, younger individuals to the vice-presidential level. The branch network, which consisted of three-quarters of the personnel, continued to report to the Senior Vice-president (Branch Operations), although some of his other responsibilities were removed. The branches were grouped in regions, each headed by a regional vice-president to whom the branch managers reported. The Senior Vice-president was the link between the branch network and the product areas. For example, product vice-presidents set goals for branch performance in their business plans, which were negotiated with the Senior Vice-president (Branch Operations) to ensure that they were achievable by the branches. Product vice-presidents interacted informally with the branch managers but there was no formal reporting relationship.

One final component of Leclaire's change strategy was the use of symbolic signals to underscore the new, innovative approach. He offered to process all the stock options cashed in by BCE employees in the two-week period before

Christmas 1990. Leclaire knew that the job could be done but a meeting of his senior vice-presidents started with a series of excuses why it could *not*. Leclaire announced that senior managers were paid to act, not to find excuses for not acting. Furthermore, the deal represented $500,000 (Canadian) in profit. If it was scuttled, budgets would be cut by an equivalent amount. Suddenly the mood changed, and solutions were found.

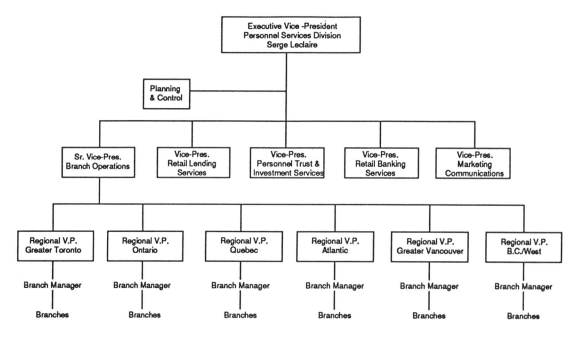

Figure 1 *Montreal Trust: Personnel Services Division (1990)*

It soon became clear, however, that the new structure was not working. The Senior Vice-president (Branch Operations) retained too much power and proved unable to adapt to the new culture and delegate autonomy. His ambivalence concerning the new strategy started to compromise Leclaire's credibility. While branch managers claimed they liked the idea of Leclaire's changes, their mode of dealing with the Senior Vice-president continued in the traditional manner. Just before Christmas 1990, the position was abolished, the individual subsequently left the company, and Leclaire was free to interact directly with the branch network (Figure 2). It was time for the next stage of the programme — giving more autonomy and accountability to branch managers and getting closer to the clients.

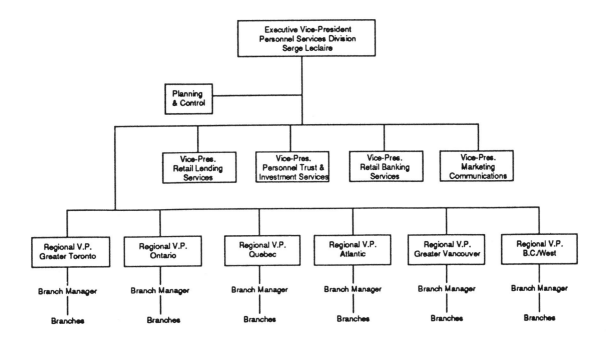

Figure 2 *Montreal Trust: Personnel Services Division (1990)*

As PSD further developed its niche strategy, it became clear that different branches, with different types of customer, had different needs. Leclaire wanted to engender more entrepreneurialism and autonomy in the branches to allow managers to respond to these needs. In 1992, branch managers started to engage in making 3-year budget forecasts. They were given guidelines concerning performance expectations but then expected to develop the means to reach their goals by tailoring promotions and products to the needs of the catchment area. To provide the necessary support, these managers were given a lot of help in using the sophisticated database and formulating business plans. Gradually, the branch managers responded to their new responsibilities.

Another change that Leclaire made at the end of 1992 was to return to a functional structure. The product groups had helped to shake things up, but now they were hindering the development of a 'package' of services. The individual product groups were merged into one, where managers worked as a team to offer clients the appropriate range and mix of services tailored to their particular situation. In addition, the number of regions were cut from six to four.

By 1994, although he was still fine-tuning one niche strategy, Leclaire felt most of his change programme had been achieved. Divisional profits, after evaporating in 1991, had increased to $20 million (Canadian) by 1993. Loan losses were down from a high of $17 million to $10 million, non-performing loans had been cut by 50 per cent, and products per client had doubled during the same period.

Questions

- What do you think of Leclaire's attempts to change the culture?
- How will the new structure help realize the strategic changes?

Mrs Fields' Cookies

A useful way to discuss Mrs Fields' Cookies is to compare the benefits of using technology with a franchise system. Before doing so, it is important to clarify Debbi Fields' goals in order to show how technology helps to achieve them. They are as follows: maintain the corporate culture; maintain an informal communication system; keep a simple structure; no franchises or licensing; maintain consistent product quality and service across an increasing number of stores, and a larger geographic area; and keep employees happy, productive, and honest.

What Technology Enabled Mrs Fields' Cookies to Accomplish

First, technology enabled management to have daily control over stores that otherwise would be impossible to achieve — the company would have to franchise. Second, it allowed the promotion of the founder's vision into parts of company that Debbi Fields had long ago outgrown her ability to reach. For example, the Day Planner incorporates Debbi Fields' hourly sales goals, suggestion selling, sampling etc. The scheduling system actually used the time she took to mix and bake cookies, ensuring the consistency of products across stores. Third, management (at all levels) did less administrative work and could be more creative and spend more time with people. This also kept headquarters staff to a minimum and reduced costs. Fourth, technology changed the skill set required in store managers — allieviating the need for skilled administrators and allowing the company to hire 'people-oriented' staff. Fifth, communication was facilitated because store managers could communicate daily with Debbi Fields and vice-versa. Also, because store managers dealt directly with senior managers, the company 'felt' flat! Finally, in-store costs were reduced since the baking system is automated and the number of throwaway cookies minimized, generating sales because the store manager spent less time doing administrative work.

© B. Poisson.

In summary, technology helped Debbi Fields achieve her goals in a way that franchising would not have. A franchise system trades off revenue/profit/flexibility for stability/control. Relationships in a franchise system are static as it is encompassed in a contract — it is difficult to alter as the market changes. Also note the cost effectiveness of this technology — only one-half of 1 per cent of revenue was spent on MIS!

Success Factors in the use of Technology

Managers need a consistent vision of what they want to accomplish with technology. What functions should be controlled? What should the organization chart look like? Managers need to know what their goals are if they are to know whether the systems are achieving them. Technology was part of the culture at Mrs Fields' Cookies and not under the sole control of the MIS function. Because it was shared by all employees, it was easier to build a collective vision of the company's future. Debbi Fields had an advantage in that she did not have a pre-existing system to deal with — there was no empire to dismantle. Management used off-the-shelf technology (which helped reduce costs). It is not the gadgets that make a system unique, but the vision of how they can be used to manage the company. Technology is an on-going process. Managers should be constantly looking for more ways to automate functions and processes (if a machine can do it, a machine should do it) and processing information in a way that allows managers to make better decisions more easily.

Mrs Fields' Cookies (B)

The success of Mrs Fields' Cookies continued. Revenue for 1985 and 1986 was $72.6 million and $87 million respectively. Earnings were a healthy 18.5 per cent after tax. By 1987, Mrs Fields' Cookies was operating 543 stores in six countries including Australia and Japan, had revenue of $104 million, earnings of $18 million and employed 4,500 people. The company had gone public on London's Unlisted Securities Market, with an initial price of 140 pence/share ($2.46 US/share). British investors, however, showed some reservations about the company by buying only 16 per cent of the offered shares. Later in the year, Mrs Fields' Cookies purchased *La Petite Boulangerie*, a chain of 119 bakery shops, from Pepsico for $15 million.

Both Randi and Debbi Fields, as well as outside analysts, attributed much of their success to their strategic use of technology. First, the systems were implemented with a strong focus on people. All software was written to be as simple as possible for the end-user, was menu-driven, and included on-line tutorials. 'Computer phobias' were eradicated by giving all employees a set of four computer games so they could familiarize themselves with personal computers while having fun. Training was provided by internal employees as it was believed that people learnt better from their peers in a relaxed environment. Additional classes were scheduled regularly to increase skills and Randi Fields set an impressive example by being a dedicated user. Support for ironing out bugs was provided by a 'Guru Department', an adjunct to the MIS department, where computer whizzes and hackers with titles such as 'Senior Computer Geek' provided immediate support to end users.

However, the main reason that the implementation was such a success is that it provided everybody with the information that they required to carry out their side of the business. Store managers embraced the technology wholeheartedly, and instead of perceiving it as intrusive, viewed it as a valuable tool. It freed up store managers from routine administrative tasks and allowed them to concentrate on managing their people, serving customers, and thinking up creative new ways to increase store sales. Furthermore, the feedback information was extremely useful, as it allowed store managers to see on an hour-by-hour basis how they were doing and react accordingly. Since part of their salary was based on store revenues, this was seen as a definite advantage.

From a corporate standpoint, technology allowed Mrs Fields' Cookies to achieve four major objectives. First, it ensured that every store was run in the same way that Debbi Fields ran her first store in Palo Alto, since it incorporated her standards and beliefs. For instance, the hourly sales goals were used to elicit action. When sales per customer were below average, the system would produce a prompt asking, 'Are you doing enough suggestive selling?' If overall sales were down, the system would suggest that they should be doing 'sample selling' on the street. The scheduling system was based on the time it took Debbi Fields to mix and bake cookies herself, and hence set the same standard for all stores. In Randi Fields' terms, technology allowed them to 'leverage' Debbi Fields and her knowledge.

Secondly, the communication system enabled Debbi Fields to be in constant contact with her store managers, deal with problems quickly and provide them with feedback (both positive and negative) immediately. She was able to constantly project her vision into the stores without having to be there. Initially, however, this part of the implementation was not a success. Debbi Fields found herself inundated with phone messages with no way to skim through them quickly or classify them by order of importance. Often, the phone-mail system was full and would not even receive any more messages. It was not the idea that was wrong, however, just the implementation. Debbi Fields continued to use the phone-mail message system to communicate with her managers, and they could use it to send urgent messages to her. However, for more routine messages the store managers sent notes on an electronic mail system. They were guaranteed a response within 48 hours.

The third direct benefit of the technology is that it allowed Mrs Fields' Cookies to maintain day-to-day control over an increasing number of stores, in a wider geographic area that would have been impossible to achieve otherwise. All information from the stores went directly to seven store controllers in Park City. These individuals could see what every location was doing every day in terms of sales, staffing, training, hiring, repairs and inventory levels — they had a 'real-time' view of operations. Their responsibility was to review all numbers daily and spot any anomalies. For instance, were store sales holding constant? Was the relationship between inventory reports, batches baked, and were the sales reports in line? When anomalies were spotted, the store controllers did not deal with any chain of command — they went directly to the store managers, and solved all problems at the local level. The offshoot of the system is that it has enabled Mrs Fields' Cookies to keep communication lines flat.

Finally, the technology saved Mrs Fields' Cookies a lot of money. Randi Fields estimated that they added 3 per cent to 5 per cent to pre-tax margins. These savings were due to store efficiencies (less waste, better scheduling, etc.) and the ability to keep headquarters staff to a minimum. Mrs Fields' Cookies had one headquarters position for every five stores, compared to the industry average of one such position for every two or three stores. Randi Fields believed that without these systems, headquarters staff would have grown to over 200, instead of 115.

Randi Fields had no intention of stopping here. He continued to adhere to his philosophy that if a machine can do it, a machine should do it. He was developing a system to combine the sales projection and inventory reports and automatically order all supplies for each store. Store managers will simply have to review and approve the orders, which will appear on their screens. Randi was also planning an Artificial Intelligence system to deal with exception reporting.

> Eventually, even the anomalies become normal. The exceptions themselves, and a person's response to them, assume a pattern. Why not have the computer watch the person for a while? Then the machine can say, 'I have found an anomaly. I've been watching you, and I think this is what you would do. Shall I do it for you, yes or no?' (Randi Fields)

Mrs Fields' Cookies' goal was, then, to automate as many processes and functions as possible as the company continued to grow. Its growth plans include opening new MFC stores, as well as developing a new line of bakery shops to complement the recent acquisition of *La Petite Boulangerie*.

Questions

- What was Mrs Fields' recipe for success?
- How can she sustain it as the company grows and diversifies?

Source Material

Advertising Age, 'All the chips fall into place for Mrs Fields', 2 April 1984.
Business Week, 'Honey, what do you say we start our own company?', 15 September 1986.
Forbes, 'Succeeding by failing', 25 June 1990.
Fortune, 'Tough cookies?', 13 February 1989.
Inc., 'Mrs Fields' secret ingredient', October 1987.
Inc., 'Use technology to manage people', May 1990.

Inc., 'A tale of two companies', July 1984.
New York Times, 'One smart cookie', 25 October 1987.
New York Times, 'Mrs Fields' french deal', 16 December 1988.
Sales and Marketing Management, 'Some awfully smart cookies', May 1988.
Wall Street Journal, 'Fresh cookie stores feel bite as snack food market shifts', 24 April 1986.
Wall Street Journal, 'Cookie canard', 24 July 1986.
Wall Street Journal, 'Mrs Fields Inc.', 15 February 1989.
Washington Post, 'Cookie czar launches an all-oat attack on unhealthy eating', 16 February 1989.

Automakers of Canada

The Autoworkers case is set in Canada but it could apply to almost any automobile manufacturing plant in North America or Western Europe. It offers a particularly graphic view of cultural characteristics that can be found, albeit in more genteel forms, in many other companies. While the automobile industry is particularly noted for its macho culture, similar forms of behaviour exist in a wide variety of companies. Culture is almost inevitably a barrier to change and it is one key factor that change agents have to take into account whether they work in a car plant, a bank, a high-tech firm, or a university. Automakers thus makes for an entertaining and dramatic look at a common problem: how to change culture in order to support strategic change. Students can wrestle with these ideas by being asked to provide an action plan for the consultants, following which the instructor can reveal the complexity and difficulty of the consultants' task with reference to the B case.

There are three underlying reasons behind the lack of success at T Plant. The first concerns the discrepancy between the expectations and goals of the consultants and those of the managers. The consultants had brought with them not only a set of techniques for organizational design but their own set of assumptions about the nature of work, information, organization, technology and people. They represented a *goal*-oriented philosophy where employees and managers were expected to behave in ways that would enable them to achieve certain objectives, rather than act according to predefined *roles*. The existing culture forced specific roles on individuals as they struggled with the pressures (Figure 1) and, so, the consultants wanted to change it. The plant manager, however, saw the existing culture as problematic *only* to the extent that it prevented the realization of the explicit goals of improved quality and reduced costs.

The second reason concerns the transition role that the consultants wanted the managers to adopt — that of students while they were taught a new way of doing things. The consultants expected the managers to engage in a process of self-examination and make fundamental changes in the way they managed. The managers, however, were not aware of the need for such profound change.

Based on: Westley, F., "The Eye of the Needle: Cultural and Personal Transformation in a Traditional Organization", *Human Relations*, 43(3), 273-93, 1990. All quotations taken and tables adapted from this article.

T PLANT'S TRADITIONAL ASSUMPTIONS	QWL CONSULTANT'S ASSUMPTIONS
Role simplicity	Role complexity
Managing technology	Managing people
Information as power	Information as process
'One Big Brain'	'Many Little Brains'
Controlling people	Controlling systems
Segmentation	Integration
Competition	Cooperation
Coercion	Participation

Figure 1 *Assumptions of managers and consultants*

The change in culture and the role of student were not intuitively obvious means for arriving at their explicit end of improved quality. Also, the role of student was poorly grasped because such a contemplative orientation did not suit the action focus of an assembly line organization, and the resulting anxiety was experienced as a loss of control, status or direction.

Third, the strategic refocus on quality was handed down in a directive from Detroit, but with no acknowledgement that, if quality was to become a real priority, concessions would have to be made in the form of lower productivity targets. There was no realization that the transition period would involve some adjustment problems as managers and workers learned new ways of operating. As a result, plant management experienced no respite from the grinding pressure of numbers. In fact, the wider competitive pressures meant that new demands — in the form of cost control and improved quality — were *added to* existing productivity targets. Accordingly, there was no room for manoeuvre in modifying reward systems, allowing time for participation to solve problems, investing in training, etc. In fact, management was under such pressure that it needed results — fast!

As a result of these factors, the change programme was experienced as a nightmare where the safety of the old culture was challenged by one which promoted participation instead of power; cooperation instead of competition; contemplation instead of action. Negative perceptions and the lack of results further inhibited the transition (see Figure 2). No culture can supplant an old culture without the loss of some cherished aspects: while some employees were willing to relinquish some abusive behaviour, many expressed regrets over the loss of excitement. Cultural assumptions are interlocking, complex and tenaciously held and the culture at T Plant, while often dysfunctional, was nonetheless tailored to the product and reinforced by the self-selection of organizational members. Auto firms still attract a large number of workers not just because they need a job, but because they love cars and what they symbolize. That the culture is tough and competitive is simultaneously resented and enjoyed — to tamper with it strikes at deeply held convictions. Accordingly, due consideration must be given to an appropriate transition phase.

	Existing (role) Culture		**Transition Culture**		**Goal Culture**	
Organization level	'2×4' management competition		committees		participative management improved quality	
Individual level	'lying, cheating, stealing' suspicion, resistance, nostalgia		'manager-shepherd' 'obedient soldier'		'good student' 'inspired followers' 'enlightened converts'	
Factors affecting change	Inhibitors: excitment	Facilitators: discontent, US directive	Inhibitors: loss of control, sense of impotence	Facilitators: internal role models, consultants	Inhibitors: culture clash	Facilitators: corporate approval, concrete results

Figure 2 *Transition culture at Plant T*

Consideration must also be given to the supporting changes that must reinforce the cultural change. Without new reward systems, new promotional patterns, training, new targets, new authority patterns and reporting relationships, it is quickly back to 'business as usual'. This can be seen in the problems that the committees ran into in the B case.

The consultants did, however, eventually experience some success. One of the crucial mechanisms that ultimately helped them was a small group of individuals who were able to act as a bridge between the consultants and other managers. One member of the Level 1 committee was able to grasp the needs of subordinates to function in the new system.

> What happened was that the (Level 1) committee just quit following things up and the people themselves (in Levels 2 and 3) didn't know how to interpret the data, how to find out the data, or how to prioritize things in terms of the data they had. We had, in fact, to retrain people about what things meant. For example, one of the basis of this business is the percentage of first runs. When I sat down with some of my people, it turned out they weren't even aware of these percentages. The data was there but they didn't react until someone told them to. Someone said to me, 'Yeah, the guys have more time to sit around the office now'. I said it's not because they have less to do, it's because they don't know how to interpret things.

This individual was able to see his role as that of a teacher. He understood the skills that his subordinates needed to change their behaviour: information processing; group facilitation; group problem-solving; process observation, etc. This manager was finally able to grasp the role of the committees as a *school* within which he was a *student*. The consultants were able to use his *shepherding* as a bridge to individuals, enabling them to see their own interactions differently.

Another important individual was a successful production manager who had been with the company for years. He was seen as a tough manager, dedicated and loyal, who got things done. When he first encountered the idea of participative management, he developed a strong belief in it as a principle, although he had previously exemplified the 2×4 style.

> It makes a lot of sense to me that we should all treat people with respect. Why should people be afraid to come to work? Why should they be afraid to lose their jobs? Why should they live in fear all the time?

At the same time, he was highly critical of the new style and felt his own attempts to implement it had largely been unsuccessful. He disliked the lack of feedback, felt that the suppression of emotion was somehow dishonest, and did not believe that the programme would necessarily lead to improved quality and productivity. Despite his private lack of conviction, he had by his example convinced his subordinates that it was safe to act in accordance with the dictates of the programme. His shift showed a marked improvement both in productivity and morale when compared with its past record and the other shift.

He's like that -- he has changed so much that he has turned us all into followers. We have believed it so much that we are reacting differently.

In this case, imitation, even without comprehension, had demonstrated that the new style could get results. In this case, however, the student/teacher role was entirely absent: in its place was the image of the obedient, disciplined *soldier*, unquestioning of authority, leading his inspired and devoted troops.

T plant had some success with its move towards a new management style through the use of these internal role models. The unions never did participate in this particular programme, although the change in the behaviour of the foremen improved relations between them and the workers. The transition was also helped by an increasing awareness in Detroit that quality could not be simply grafted on to existing objectives but had to be grounded in company-wide modifications and support. As a result, the larger company did make some headway towards quality, which translated into a more respectable bottom line, at least in the short term. Losses that exceeded $3.3 billion between 1980 and 1982 were transformed into record profits in 1983 and 1984. Costs were cut and the breakeven point was reduced. How much of this success was to due to fundamental changes in the company and how much was due to the end of the recession is a moot point. In any event, the euphoria didn't last long since, by 1991, the accummulated losses of the US car firms had reached $7.6 billion.

Automakers of Canada (B)

The committees met over a two-year period and, while they did solve some specific operational problems, they made little progress on the overall organizational transformation. As a result, both plant management and consultants became impatient.

The plant manager was frustrated with a programme that had little impact on either costs or quality. He attributed the failure to a lack of performance control — in his mind, the supervisors were becoming too slack because of the new participative approach. While Detroit had insisted on quality, they had not eased up on their demands for productivity and cost-cutting, nor had they allowed for any transition or learning period during which new behaviours, processes and procedures were assimilated and implemented. He was still subject to the pressures of the old system in addition to those of the planned new system. The consultants were equally frustrated. They felt that plant management was inconsistent in communicating its support for programme goals; rewards for changing behaviour were negligible; there was no punishment for those who ignored quality directives; and training for participants was inadequate. The consultants also felt that management's desire for 'discipline and control' was counterproductive because it generated distrust.

The committees had been set up in the context of a QWL programme designed to meet the consultants' definition of the problem, not the managers' assessment of their situation. As a result, they were operating in a vacuum because little else in the plant had changed to support them. Accordingly, all committees encountered problems.

Level 1

The frustration of the Level 1 managers that resulted from the lack of progress caused them to define the new style as mere window dressing. Their

Based on (and all quotations from): Westley, F., "The Eye of the Needle: Cultural and Personal Transformation in a Traditional Organization", *Human Relations*, 43(3), 273-93, 1990.

abandonment of their previous jungle-fighter management style resulted in feelings of impotence and ineffectiveness. They had moved away from the old culture but had not yet made the transition into a new one. Disenchanted with the lack of results, they began to wonder if the changes were counterproductive. Conditions on the shopfloor were perceived as chaotic and out of control, while quality and quantity were suffering.

> Right now we are concentrating on patting people on the back but it's tough when someone isn't whipping them. Things get dropped. They don't share our priorities. The main issue for me is: are they going to pick up that ball by themselves or not. Right now I see a slacking off period. I'd like to know if it's temporary or not. If I grab that 2×4 I could make them do it. I don't — I'm not grabbing it which is hard for me. The question is, will they pick up the ball?

Level 2

Level 2 managers had had to assume more authority as Level 1 withdrew. Despite the fact that they had demanded the increased autonomy, they felt frightened and lost. What Level 1 saw as delegation, Level 2 saw as being abandoned.

> The whole pullback of Level 1 happened much too fast, first of all there were a bunch of people out there dictating everything with their radios and suddenly they just turned it completely over, they were all over the place one day and they had gone the next. You couldn't find them if you wanted them. Sure .... people wanted to do their own job, but you don't take a child out of the playpen and put him in the street all at once. They should have done it more gradually, one item at a time. Each week maybe, they could explain one aspect of the job, what was needed within what constraint, how to go about it and gradually turned things over. You can't just dump things on people who aren't used to it.

Level 2 managers were particularly ill-prepared for their new role. First, they were supposed to collect the system-wide information that would allow them to identify the source and location of quality problems. Unfortunately, the sudden abdication of Level 1 had left them with an information gap. There was a joke among them that the only way to find out what was going on was to ask the sweeper who cleaned the offices of the Level 1 committee. Second, even when the necessary information was available, they were unable to process it in a way that enabled them to identify and locate problems. Finally, for these managers to fix problems 'on the spot', there would have to be significant changes in processes and procedures. For example, authority had to be delegated to allow them to take the necessary action; functional barriers had to be broken down to allow people to come together; and the emphasis on productivity had to be reduced. Even if these managers had the power to stop the line to fix a problem, they would be unlikely to use it: stopping the line reduced productivity, which was directly reflected in bonuses and pay!

Level 3

Many Level 3 participants were hardly aware of the change effort due to: a lack of exposure to the consultants; the failure to provide resources to support the change effort; a lack of rewards for changed behaviour; and the inability to attend meetings due to a lack of personnel.

> Our superintendent goes along with participative management until things are bad and then it's back to 2×4. I've seen him spend two months building up credibility for the programme and then he turns around the next day and he's saying the programme is a pile of shit because it's to his advantage to cancel it (the meeting) that day. So the guys say, 'Ah, fuck it.'

They perceived the change to be erratic — some managers were participatory, others were not, and individuals changed from day to day.

> Well, first of all, they need consistency. They can't keep changing from 2×4 to participative management every day. The way things stand now, people don't want to take responsibility because they're liable to come right back and take it away. We've all been handed things and told, 'that's yours' and then we do it one way and then just because it's not the way the boss would have done it, you get told off about it sooner or later.... Right now people don't know where they're going.

The attempt to form quality circles also foundered because of a lack of support. Participants were supposed to bridge departments in a plant previously characterized by high walls around them. Managers lacked the motivation, skills, resources and time to carry out the multi-disciplinary interactions now demanded of them. This severely restricted their ability to solve problems at this level. When matters were passed up to Level 2, these managers were overworked and ill-prepared, so problems did not get solved there either.

As a result of these problems, the change effort was perceived simply as a new way of achieving old ends: a new tool to 'push the numbers' or spy on other people. Groups who couldn't get any work done in the new format would have to 'fudge' some kind of progress report or suffer the consequences. Meetings were yet another forum for people to 'look good' and were used by superiors to catch out subordinates. Consensus decision-making was a means for blocking initiatives and passing the buck.

Questions

- Why did the change effort have such little success?
- What would you have done differently?
- Where would you go from here?

A New Strategy at ICI

This is a relatively complex case which is best employed towards the end of the course when students have a better grasp on the complexity of strategic change. It is a versatile case that can be used to explore the role of leadership, culture, power, and the board in strategic change, as well as the implementation of global strategies. I have found it useful to ask students to prepare an action plan for John Harvey Jones, regarding how he should manage ICI's culture and how he should structure the Main Board. Students then find it interesting to read the second case, *Preparing ICI for Change*, to see what Harvey-Jones actually did, followed by a discussion of the issues raised in it. Instructors can also use the case to compare the situation of boards in the UK with those in North America, where their composition and responsibilities are somewhat different. Boards in North America tend to focus far more power in the hands of the CEO (see, for example, *Barbarians at the Gate* by B. Burrough and J. Helyar) who are subject to short term pressures, particularly share prices. Other countries such as Japan, with its very different system of financial markets, and Germany, where management and unions 'co-determine' decisions, can also be factored into the comparison.

Despite Harvey-Jones' achievements and the rosy picture when Denys Henderson took over, by 1990 sales and profits were falling once again, leading to demands from the Main Board for further rationalization. Henderson initially avoided any major divestments, but in February 1991 he announced a reappraisal of the company to see if the strategy of the 1980s was still appropriate for the 1990s. The company was reorganized into seven international divisions, and a major streamlining plan was implemented — more than 5,000 jobs were cut. In July, ICI announced that pre-tax profits for the first six months of 1991 were 31 per cent lower than in the same period of 1990. The announcement followed the purchase of a 2.8 per cent stake in ICI by Hanson (a conglomerate known for its 'unfriendly' acquisitions and subsequent asset-stripping). While no takeover attempt was made, the share purchase did spark a flurry of activity as ICI tried both to improve its financial position and secure public and media condemnation of a takeover. In 1993, ICI was the subject of a 'demerger' as pharmaceuticals and biotechnology were separated to form a new company.

Preparing ICI for Change

In September 1981, John Harvey-Jones was voted Chairman for a five-year term commencing April 1982. He had a five-year plan for turning around ICI. He allocated the first year to changing the Board; the second and third years were devoted to the clarification of the strategies for the operating units; and the fourth and fifth years were aimed at changing people and their attitudes while pursuing these strategies.

John Harvey-Jones in the Driver's Seat

Following his appointment, Harvey-Jones set about meeting with his executive directors to discuss the role of the Main Board. The following principles (many of which had been recommended as far back as 1973) emerged: (a) the Chairman should have a greater degree of executive responsibility (the harshness of the term 'chief executive officer' was softened somewhat by the use of the term 'principal executive officer'); (b) the Main Board should be reduced in size; (c) divisional chairmen should have greater responsibility; (d) the style of the Main Board would have to change. Harvey-Jones had gained significant power, at least in ICI terms, with the allocation of portfolios; the right to recommend appointments to the Board; the power to recommend directors' remuneration; and the termination of appointments (which was never used).

Harvey-Jones replaced three British executive directors with American, German and Japanese nonexecutive directors and reduced the number of executive directors from eleven to eight. Several layers of staff were cut to create a more direct link between the Main Board and operations. Profit and operating responsibility was decentralized to divisional chairmen, leaving the eight executive directors to concentrate on the performance of the group as a whole. Harvey-Jones simplified the matrix structure of the Main Board

All quotations taken from Pettigrew, A.M., *The Awakening Giant: Continuity and Change in Imperial Chemical Industries*, Oxford: Basil Blackwell, 1985.

somewhat, reduced directors' loads from three to two areas, and ended the Policy Groups. In this way, he ended the tradition of advocacy and pulled together a closely knit team that would develop a vision for the company.

This streamlined group of directors developed a strategy that would: decrease dependency on commodities, while improving its efficiency in these sectors; increase the proportion of the company's business in high added-value products; extend its presence in Western Europe and the USA; seek out high-growth markets; and make strategic acquisitions in line with these objectives.

ICI withdrew from certain businesses, notably polythene, and combined four mainstream chemical divisions — agricultural, fibres, Mond (explosives), and petrochemicals and plastics — into a single organizational entity, called the Chemicals and Polymers Group. It had a number of advantages. It provided a mechanism for achieving economies of scale and, if necessary, making further cuts. Second, it uncoupled the bulk of commodities from newer speciality businesses. Third, as a separately incorporated subsidiary, ICI had the option of divesting it should that need arise. The aim in these sectors was to achieve maximum economies of scale.

ICI started to increase investment in products where it could add value and benefit from premium pricing and growth. It was in these areas that globalization was most important, particularly in pharmaceuticals — a £1 billion business that earned over £270 million in profits in 1985, with an average annual growth rate of 27 per cent. It became a truly international business: by 1987 40 per cent of ICI's pharmaceutical products were manufactured in the USA and only 5 per cent in the UK. Globalization was applied to other products. In 1983 a new grouping of speciality chemicals was created by drawing together the USA, the UK and Europe under a single management group. A similar grouping was created for advanced materials (mainly for use in electronics) and polyurethanes.

Three new principal executive officers were appointed to head these groups. They had the same status as UK divisional chairmen and all three were located overseas. A series of acquisitions was made to reinforce the strategy. Beatrice Chemicals, a US firm, was acquired in 1984 for $750 million to complement the specialities and advanced materials groups. This acquisition led to the creation of an acquisitions team based at Millbank. It was headed by Denys Henderson who was to succeed Harvey-Jones in 1987. This team organized a $580 million purchase of The Glidden Co, a US paint manufacturer, which made ICI the largest paint supplier in the world with sales of over £1 billion.

Getting from Here to There

Although Harvey-Jones finally assumed the driver's seat at ICI, it had not been easy. His efforts had started as early as 1973. The failure of the Organization Committee had not deterred him from continuing to seek change. He abandoned his attempt to influence the existing Chairman (Jack Callard, who was due to step down in March 1975) and, instead, waited until the next Chairman was appointed. In the meantime, he used his Board responsibility 'to legitimately roam all over the place . . . . in a fairly structured way in order to get some of the real dissatisfactions of ordinary guys with the performance of the Board recognized'. During 1974, he encouraged a number of counter-cultural changes. He set up a room at the Millbank headquarters where:

> anybody could put up a chart to bring the bad news to the attention of the Board without having to stand up and say boo! . . . . I got a number of studies done of views of where the Board was going . . . . and I started a real effort to try and get the staff in Millbank to . . . . put pressure on the Board.[1]

He set up a Directors' Advisory Committee for Petrochemicals — the first mechanism to pull together a group of division chairmen.

He also began to meet with Stewart Dudley, an internal OD consultant, 'to prepare a strategy for opening up a discussion with the Main Board' about ICI's problems. They targeted their attempts at the next Chairman, whom they expected to be Rowland Wright. Dudley wrote a paper called 'A Look at ICI in 1974' to be used as the vehicle to draw the Board into a serious discussion about organization matters.

> Our plan was to influence a group of directors by going to them individually with the 'ICI in 1974' note, rewriting it if they didn't agree with it, but slowly building up a note that was acceptable to a critical mass of directors on an individual level. We then planned to give that note to Rowland Wright immediately after his appointment [announced in 1974], but before he formally became Chairman in April 1975.[2]

This carefully planned tactic went astray when Harvey-Jones' secretary mistakenly circulated Dudley's draft to the Chairman and Board. The result was, in Harvey-Jones' words:

> the most fantastic explosion — absolutely marvellous. The Chairman sent for me white with rage, lost his temper, and commanded that I withdraw it, and demanded I fire Stewart. I said: 'No way, poor devil. I've asked him to do this. If you don't like it, fire me!' That was a real breakthrough in its own way but it hadn't been designed. It meant

we were able to get Ron Mercer (an external OD consultant) to the Chairman. It also meant we were able to raise the pain level on the Board so that when Roland Wright became Chairman he did his trips around the Company to talk to people at various levels, and this again increased the pain level and began to open up the possibility of change.[3]

Callard was shocked by the report. 'Much of what is said in it is contrary to the impression I have gained travelling at home and abroad amongst the ICI Organization . . . . Are you, or whoever, trying to tell me that my 39 years has been totally wasted? Are you seeking to destroy my faith? Or are you making a bid for a new era launched by enlightened men?'.[4] Mercer was, despite this, invited to present his diagnosis to the Board. He remarked: 'There were various degrees of belief and disbelief, but this helped to motivate what Rowland Wright was going to do when he took over.' The minutes of the meeting, however, were not so optimistic.

> An improvement in the general area covered by the discussion was most likely to be achieved by a fairly low-profile approach from the top, aiming at gradual rather than sudden or dramatic change.[5]

Nevertheless, change had at least become a legitimate topic of discussion. The new Chairman was persuaded to go into the divisions to take the company's pulse. He took the executive directors away for a two-day informal meeting to discuss ICI's structure and operation, and followed it up with taskforces to examine organization change. He set up a Board Resource Group consisting of Harvey-Jones, Dudley and Mercer, 'to provide personal support to the Chairman when he is faced with the personal risk of validating new behaviour and actions'.[6]

In the meantime, an informal group of division chairmen had formed as a defensive manoeuvre against centralized personnel policies. It was not recognized but, seeing the Board discuss the possibility of change, the division chairmen began to try to convince the Board that these changes had their support. In 1977, this group became part of the formal hierarchy and an annual conference was set up to allow executive directors to meet with the division chairmen, chief executives of overseas subsidiaries, and functional managers to discuss the policy, aims, and organization of ICI. These meetings became legitimate mechanisms used by the change caucus to mobilize support.

The Board continued to agonize about change but never enacted it. By 1977, however, new people were coming on to the Board, who were in favour of change but who were, by no means, uniform in their priorities. One stream of thinking emphasized the importance of marketing and commercial skills versus the technical skills of older generations of ICI management. Another stream, personified by Harvey-Jones who became a deputy chairman in 1978, recognized the importance of globalization and saw that changes in the commercial sphere would require a rethinking of the entire organization and culture of ICI.

In 1980, ICI declared a loss — its first since its formation in 1926 — of £20 million on sales of around £6 billion, and reduced its dividends for the first time since the 1930s. The problems had been caused by a number of factors. First, the heavy dependence on the UK economy had backfired as inflation increased, the UK customer base collapsed, sterling became increasingly overvalued, and labour productivity declined. These domestic problems exacerbated the effects of the worldwide recession that followed the 1970s oil crisis. Second, the massive capital investment of the 1960s and 1970s had been pumped into the production of commodity chemicals (such as plastics and petrochemicals), which were particularly vulnerable to cyclical fluctuations. Despite a decision by the Board in 1970 to reduce the company's dependence on commodities and increase its investment in speciality products, the distribution of the business was unchanged ten years later.

The Reorientation of ICI

It was the crisis provoked by this loss that led to Harvey-Jones' appointment and finally provoked sufficient momentum for strategic change. When Denys Henderson took over from Harvey-Jones in 1987, ICI was a profitable company once again with more than £10 billion in sales and £1 billion in profit (Table 1). It was offering shareholders a 20 per cent pre-tax return on their money, which was considerably better than its recent performance. Between 1982 and 1986, return on assets increased from 7 to 19 per cent; return on chemical sales increased from 5 to 10.5 per cent; and earnings per share went from 29 to 92 pence. Sales of bulk products dropped from 52 per cent of total sales to 46 per cent in 1985, while non-commodity chemicals increased from 38 per cent to 48 per cent of sales and generated 64 per cent of profits. Dependence on UK sales was down from 37 per cent to 25 per cent, while the US proportion of sales was up from 15 per cent in 1980 to 22 per cent in 1985. Harvey-Jones was voted the most impressive industrialist for three successive years by Britain's business elite.

Table 1   *ICI, financial performance, 1970-90*

	Sales (£ million)	Net Income (£ million)
1970	1,462	86.7
1971	1,524	19.9
1972	1,694	75.5
1973	2,166	177.4
1974	2,955	232.1
1975	3,129	171.0
1976	4,135	245.0
1977	4,663	290.0
1978	4,533	301.0
1979	5,368	441.0
1980	5,715	(20.0)
1981	6,581	186.0
1982	7,358	145.0
1983	8,256	378.0
1984	9,909	585.0
1985	10,725	512.0
1986	10,136	557.0
1987	11,123	760.0
1988	11,699	837.0
1989	13,171	1057.0
1990	12,906	670.0

Source: 1970-74 *Moody's*, 1975, vol. 1
       1975-80 *Moody's*, 1981, vol. 1
       1981-83 *Moody's*, 1984, vol. 1
       1984-90 *Moody's*, 1991, vol. 1

Questions

- What is your opinion of John Harvey-Jones' actions?
- What sources of power did he use to realize his strategy?

Notes

1. Pettigrew, A. M., *The Awakening Giant Continuity and Change in Imperial Chemical Industries*, Oxford, England: Basil Blackwell, 1985 p. 396.

2. Ibid.

3. Ibid.: 397.

4. Ibid.

5. Ibid.: 399.

6. Ibid.: 401.

Source Material

Industry Week, 'Making change happen', 47-8, 18 July 1988.
Management Today, 'The legacy of Harvey-Jones', 35-88, January 1987.
Management Today, 'Matrix management muddles', p. 24, June 1991.
Pettigrew, A.M., *Some limits of executive power in creating strategic change*, paper presented at the Symposium on the Functioning of Executive Power, Case Western Reserve University, Cleveland, 1984.
Pettigrew, A. M., *The Awakening Giant Continuity and Change in Imperial Chemical Industries*, Oxford, England Basil Blackwell, 1985.
Pink, A.I.H., 'Strategic leadership through corporate planning at ICI', *Long Range Planning*, 21(1): 18-25, 1988.

PART II   MOBILIZING CHANGE: THE ROLE OF POWER

Introduction

This part provides a greater understanding of how power and politics feature in strategic change. Power is defined broadly, as a force that influences outcomes. It is important that students understand that power is context-specific, relational and dynamic. In other words, you may have power in one situation but not in another, over one person but not over another, in one time period but not another. Power sources are varied. They include rewards, sanction, authority and position, affiliation and political access, charisma, referent power, credibility, information, expertise, control over equipment and other resources, group support, and the ability to control uncertainty. In general, these sources can be divided into two broad categories: those based on dependency (that is, the control of scarce and valued resources); and those based on legitimacy. These power sources can be used either to defeat opposition or to prevent it from arising in the first place. Politics is, very simply, the process whereby power is put to use: if power is a currency, politics refers to the way you spend it.

The aim of these broad definitions is to help students understand the varied and often hidden ways in which power works. It also avoids the use of moral terminology which can, by reducing objectivity, hamper students from making an insightful study of the phenomenon. It should be stressed that power can be used for good and evil, for common interest as well as self-interest, and for legitimate and illegitimate ends. At the same time, it is important that students realize the ethical implications of the use of power.

The material has been selected for both its critical and pragmatic approach. The first two chapters, by Kotter and by Sadler, provide a glimpse of the political aspects of organizational life. The Hardy chapter is particularly important in framing the concept of power that underpins the book. It discusses four different dimensions of power and, in so doing, illuminates the hidden ways in which power is used to protect self interest. The first dimension is visible, decision making power which students should have little difficulty understanding. The second relates to nondecision making, of which students will have more difficulty in making sense. I find that a useful approach is to ask them to prepare one-page examples which can be discussed in class as well as checked by the instructor. The third dimension refers to the management of meaning — the use of power to shape attitudes. 'Northville', 'Midville', and the 'Tobacco Firms' provide examples of this type of power. Instructors can, if they wish, take this discussion outside the realm of the organization to look at it at the societal level. Noam Chomsky's work (*Manufacturing Consent*) is particularly relevant on this point. The fourth dimension introduces the way in which power works without being actively or consciously mobilized. The dimensions of power can also be used to explore the role of women in business. While gender is not an explicit focus of the book, cases like Daniel, Crown Corporation, and MSP can be used to illustrate these issues.

The chapter by Gray and Ariss links power and politics to the strategic choices that are taken at various stages of the organization's life cycle. This is a useful chapter to illustrate the political aspects of strategy making. The last two chapters in this part tackle two particular issues: empowerment and ethics. Leiba and Hardy address the specific issue of empowerment, which has become a buzz-word in contemporary management circles. A more critical reading of the prescriptive literature reveals its underlying assumptions and helps to explain why some employees do not experience empowerment as positively as the literature says they should. It also explains why some unions have adopted a very negative approach to empowerment programmes. Bird and Hardy broaden the critical perspective by examining how power can be used against individual self-interest to bring about ethical behaviour.

The cases serve a variety of purposes. 'Crown Corporation' and 'Daniel' relate power to the individual. They provide a useful means to engage students in the political realities of organizational life. 'Northville' and 'Midville' address some of the complexity of reconciling different interest groups and the political implications of doing so. They also show how power is used to manage meaning. 'Medical Services and Products' shows how strategy making takes on political dimensions, especially when strategic initiatives are resisted by powerful players. Finally, the Tobacco Firms illustrate an explicitly political strategy that revolved around the management of meaning. All these cases can be used to highlight ethical issues associated with the use of power.

PART II CASES

Daniel and the Lions' Den

Students easily relate to this particular case. Discussions revolve around how students can read signals during the interview process to prepare them for the subsequent job. The class will typically divide into those who are comfortable with such a loose structure and those who are not. The former group tends to be optimistic about Daniel's chances; the others are less sanguine. This case also raises the role of mentors (e.g. Wilson and Elman, 'The Organizational Benefits of Mentoring' *Academy of Management Executive*, 4(4), 88-94, 1990) and the various male/female pairings. When Case B is handed out, virtually all the students will be pessimistic about Daniel's chances of survival. Most will recommend looking for alternative employment, which can be used to discuss the obligations of new employees to their employers. After Case C, students are more optimistic and will suggest the importance of meeting David, and establishing some form of objective, measurable performance evaluation. The politics of performance appraisal (Longenecker et al., 'Behind the Mask: The Politics of Employee Appraisal', *Academy of Management Executive*, 1(3), 183-93, 1987) can be pursued in the subsequent discussion. Case D brings up the question of luck and the importance of planning — had Daniel met with David when he wanted to (that is, before he received the letter), he would probably not have handled it so well because he would not have been prepared. It also shows Daniel finally displaying some political skills. It also raises the question of Daniel's ability to deal with people whom he does not respect, and who are not clearly superior in terms of authority and expertise. While it is easy to dismiss Panos because of his lack of interpersonal skills, the fact remains that Daniel does 'test' people whom he does not respect and, as a result, comes across as very threatening.

Daniel and the Lions' Den (B)

The first four months were somewhat disappointing for Daniel. First, the growing rift between Mitchell and the British lawyer created political as well as professional problems in the office. A lot of work was being paralysed by a lack of decision making on the part of senior management, many of whom were barely on speaking terms. Second, Daniel was having increasing interpersonal problems with Panos, though he felt he was doing his best to ensure that Panos 'looked good' on their projects. Third, he was doing virtually no work with David and his only major project had been with Panos. One of his closest confidants to whom he vented his frustration was Panos' secretary who was also growing increasingly impatient with her boss's inconsiderate behaviour. Through Jeanette, Daniel learned that Panos was feeling increasingly threatened by him and was also having interpersonal problems with other individuals. Daniel was reassured by this news and felt that the problem lay with Panos. He felt secure in the fact that the long hours he had put in at the office to meet the tough deadlines would serve him well. He was also proud of his decision *not* to get involved in the office politics, though he privately felt that Mitchell ought to get rid of the British lawyer.

Questions

- What should Daniel do now?
- What are his chances of survival?

Daniel and the Lions' Den (C)

Daniel decided to carry on as before and was shocked when, on the final week of the probationary period, Jeanette showed him a letter that Panos had written to David. It concerned Daniel's performance. Panos had written that Daniel needed a considerable amount of direction and had performed below expectations on Panos' latest project. While Panos did not actually recommend firing him, he did say that it had been a mistake to hire him in the first place. Bianca's assessment of his performance did not help Daniel much because they had hardly worked together.

Daniel tried to schedule his review with David who, at this point, was heavily involved in the negotiations to buy out the British lawyer. David agreed to see Daniel the following week (two days before the six-month probationary period expired), and went off on one of his trips. Later that day, Daniel was handed an envelope marked 'CONFIDENTIAL and PRIVATE'. It stated the following:

> In accordance with the terms of your contract your performance now needs to be assessed. I shall be arranging to see you within the next few days to perform such a review. Meanwhile, in accordance with Belgian law, I propose to extend your trial period for a further three months.

It had been signed by David.

Question

- What would you do now if you were Daniel?

Daniel and the Lions' Den (D)

Daniel and David finally met the following week — two days before the termination of the probationary period. David dismissed Panos' letter but said that he had little evidence which he could use to evaluate Daniel because he had not worked with him. Daniel argued two main points: (a) it was not his fault that the company had not provided him with enough work to judge his performance; and (b) he had received no warning about his inadequate performance prior to this letter. He subtly reminded David that, as a Mitchell hire, he was committed to the company and his expertise comprised exactly the type of skills they were looking for. He said that he wanted to prove that he was capable of doing a good job, and alluded to Panos' problems with other members of the Office. He proposed an arrangement whereby: his trial period would be extended for a further three months; David would guarantee to provide work of a suitable nature to allow an accurate evaluation; the work would involve David or any other manager but not Panos; and David would hold a monthly evaluation meeting with Daniel to monitor progress. The deal was discussed in the meeting, following which Daniel drew up a letter which was signed by David. He also requested that the extension of his probationary period be annulled. David told him not to worry about such little legal details — 'just do a good job and the period will lapse before you know it'. Daniel then received a project on which he worked with David. He also received two good performance ratings and, at the end of three months, was given a permanent appointment. He was subsequently promoted and, by 1992, was earning $120,000 a year.

Daniel later learned that Panos had received two official warnings about the problems caused by his lack of interpersonal skills. Panos eventually received a final warning for his 'people problems' and, as his relations with senior management deteriorated further, he started to panic. Around Christmas 1990, he sent out an unauthorized letter on the computer network to all Mitchell Offices complaining about the internal problems of the Mitchell-Europe office. He went to see Gerard (who happened to be in Brussels that week) later that same morning to resign. Gerard did not take kindly to such a critical electronic memo being sent without his approval. He told Panos that his resignation was unacceptable but that he was fired in any event. He ordered him to quit the premises by noon. Panos went to work for the British lawyer, but only stayed there a year before leaving for another job in a small consulting firm.

The British lawyer was bought out and set up another law firm in Brussels. He and Mitchell Associates were suing each other for breach of contract. David returned to the UK Office and remained good friends with Daniel, whom he occasionally called for information on EC affairs. Daniel maintained good relations with most of the people in the European Office with one exception — a senior manager who was about the same age, but with slightly less experience and training. This individual was promoted to Director and given control of the Mitchell-Europe office. He blocked Daniel's promotion and tried to get rid of him under a 'cost reduction' move. By this time, however, Daniel had found himself a new mentor — a partner in the German office called Klaus who protected him politically and promoted him publicly by insisting that Daniel work with him on important contracts.

When the new Director tried to get rid of Daniel, Klaus supported him and moved him to an important project that had been the traditional breadwinner for the office. Daniel did very well on this project, and was instrumental in winning a contract to extend the project by another four years. The new Director was fired in 1992 for running the operation into the ground after less than a year. The Mitchell network took back control of the European office, with the UK, US and French offices agreeing to fund it as a hybrid cost/profit centre. The new focus of the office was to win major contracts for the entire network as opposed to its 'go it alone' policy of the past. Several staff were laid off but Daniel was asked to stay as part of the core group. Klaus told Daniel that there would always be work for him in the German Office. Daniel is currently brushing up his German.

Question

- What advice would you give to Daniel to enhance his career plans at Mitchell?

Crown Corporation

Crown Corporation works extremely well with the chapter by Kotter. A useful place to start the discussion is with an analysis of the people on whom Antonia depends to do her job: politicians, different levels of civil servants, the Board, the Treasurer, her subordinates, and other managers. When these relationships are analyzed, it can be seen that Antonia has very little power over the different groups and, accordingly, is far more dependent on them than they are on her. For example, she has no political access to the government and probably limited credibility because she is new to the province. She has limited expertise vis-à-vis her employees and limited use of rewards and sanctions because of the union situation. The confusion concerning her position may erode the authority she can derive from her position as a manager. Her expertise and credibility in the eyes of her peers is probably limited because she is new and young. She does have some internal political access owing to the support of the Treasurer, and she may be able to control the information that goes to the Board.

The issues then become: how can she manage her dependency, and is there any way of increasing her power? At this point, students can start to make recommendations. Many suggestions may be open to debate, for example, should she go over the heads of her peers and appeal directly to the Treasurer, or will it make her look weak and/or cause a backlash? Should she become more involved in the work of her subordinates, or will it antagonize them? After discussing their pros and cons, the students' suggestions can be compared with what Antonia actually did in the B and C cases.

The B case can be handed out in class and discussed by analyzing Antonia's actions in terms of the power sources she used. With the government and civil servants, she tries to emphasize her expertise and credibility and build her political access and affiliation. With the Board, she makes use of information. As far as her staff are concerned, she tries to find non-monetary ways to reward them. The use of the Treasurer to exert pressure on her colleagues represents recourse to her political access inside the organization, and the redefinition of her job description reflects an attempt to clarify her authority and power of position. In general, she makes considerable use of referent power and adopts a non-confrontational approach, which reflects her personal style. It can be used to discuss the positive and negative ways in which power can be used.

Students can be asked to advise her at the end of the B case. Some will suggest finding another job, while others will advise her to persevere in and hopefully secure the Treasurer's position. In the latter case, students should be pushed to say how she can protect herself and disassociate herself from the new guard which is currently so out of favour. The C case shows how events unfolded.

Crown Corporation (B)

Antonia decided to adopt two strategies concerning government relations. The first concerned her own staff and their daily contact with civil servants. In trying to cement good relations with the civil servants, Antonia made a deliberate decision to keep away from the political issue of centralization. Instead, she made an effort to establish personal relationships and demonstrate, as best she could, how her department was able to provide complementary activities. She also talked to her staff to convince them that they should do as much as they could to demonstrate their professionalism and good will to the bureaucrats they dealt with. Antonia had decided that lobbying these lower level bureaucrats on the centralization issue would have little effect — even if they supported Crown Corporation's autonomy, they had no direct influence on policy decisions. On the other hand, if they were dissatisfied with Crown Corporation, it could be used as additional ammunition by senior officials to support centralization.

The second strategy concerned interactions at the senior levels. She set about trying to convince the Treasurer who, she hoped, would in turn convince his boss, the Vice-president (Finance), to adopt a less confrontational stance. She felt it was in their interests to dispel the idea that Crown Corporation was difficult to deal with. The less professional the corporation was perceived to be, the more justification existed that its financial management would be better carried out by government personnel. Antonia also thought that the brief to the Secretariat for crown corporations should be used to demonstrate the contribution Crown Corporation could make by carrying out its own debt management. The Treasurer had been responsive to Antonia's suggestions, but they had both been overtaken by other events. The President had decided to use the media to establish Crown Corporation's credibility. Some financial transactions had deliberately been realized in fiscal year 1991/92 to add $100 million (Canadian) to net income, which was expected to total $400 million. It not only represented a large increase in net income but also precluded the need for a price increase. Not surprisingly, a number of press articles had subsequently appeared extolling Crown Corporation's efficient management. The media campaign had been successful in terms of creating good publicity and public support which, in turn, might predispose the politicians to look more favourably on Crown Corporation. Civil servants in the Ministry of Finance, on the other hand, remained somewhat more sceptical. They had been annoyed by the unwillingness to disclose the extra $100 million before the accounts were made public and, as a result, had become more suspicious, and more cautious, in their subsequent approval of financial transactions.

Antonia was planning a series of presentations to the new Board members, both to educate members concerning the corporation's business and to secure support for their policies and strategies. Some managers were rather dismissive of the 'non-experts' appointed to the new Board, but these individuals were well-connected to the new government and could act either as a mechanism to secure government support or, alternatively, as a barrier. The Board's lack of expertise could work in management's favour since members would be totally dependent on them for their understanding of Crown Corporation's operations.

As far as her staff was concerned, Antonia decided to avoid a heavy handed approach and issue edicts. In the short term, she tried to use her interpersonal skills to establish a personal rapport that appealed to their sense of obligation. In the longer term, she took every opportunity to impress upon them her expertise in the very sensitive area of government relations. She tried to make them realize that if they did not succeed in convincing the government to accord Crown Corporation more financial autonomy, they would all be out of a job. Her task was, then, to protect them. In return, the more they helped her, the more secure their own careers would be. Antonia was unable to reward them in terms of salary or bonuses but she tried to involve them in decision making, show them the big picture, introduce them to government officials, and publicly acknowledge their contribution. She hoped that this delegation of responsibility would produce 'ownership' not only of their individual work but of the larger problems facing the department. In this way, she could establish a common vision.

Antonia adopted a similar approach with her peers. She tried to indicate that she understood their feelings about being shunted to one side, but that she still needed their help. Unfortunately, this 'we're all in this together' approach was less successful with this group, and attempts to negotiate concessions also proved ineffective. Antonia was forced to seek recourse to the Treasurer who, on occasion, called all the managers in and ordered them to provide the necessary support. Antonia realized that her authority needed to be clarified if she was to hold sway with this group in the long term. As a result, the Treasurer started to review all job descriptions of all managerial staff with a view to clarifying the new activities required of them. Part of this involved a plan to promote Antonia to the position of Assistant Treasurer which would increase her formal leverage over both the other managers and her own subordinates. A retreat was also organized to raise such issues as the lack of team spirit in the Treasury, the lack of adequate support for some activities, and the threat of centralization.

Since her efforts had been successful, Antonia was feeling optimistic about her prospects at Crown Corporation. In June 1992, however, the Chairman of the Board was fired by the provincial government and replaced, on an interim basis, by one of the Board members — an ex-president of Crown Corporation from the days when its Treasury operations had been minimal. The following month, the Vice-president (Finance), who had spearheaded the move to reclaim Treasury operations from the government, was replaced by his predecessor, also from the time when the government carried out most of the debt management activities. So far, the Treasurer was still at Crown Corporation, although rumours were rife that his job might also be on the line.

Questions

- What do you think of Antonia's way of dealing with the various groups?
- Would you have done anything differently?
- What should Antonia do now?

Crown Corporation (C)

In August 1992, the Vice-president (Finance) hired a group of consultants to review Treasury operations. Their report, released in October 1992, recommended that the majority of debt management be carried out by the provincial government, and the Treasury be reorganized accordingly. As a result, in November, the Treasury was downsized from 18 to 8 people: the Treasurer and two managers — one of whom was Antonia, whose department was reduced to two senior analysts and two analysts. The entire department was effectively demoted by being placed under the Comptroller (who had previously been at the same level as the Treasurer).

As events unfolded, the Treasurer was moved sidewards and Antonia was made Treasurer. Relations with the civil servants and politicians were soon improved and she found out that their intention had been only to depose the Chairman, Vice-president (Finance) and Treasurer. They had not particularly wanted to take back debt management though they ended up doing so, as a result of the reorganization carried out by the Vice-president (Finance), who had miscalculated their objectives. In other words, had the Vice-president simply moved the Treasurer, the department could have remained intact.

Questions

- Who were the different interest groups in and around Crown Corporation?
- What were their goals?
- How did those groups and their goals change?

Northville Area Health Authority

The Northville and Midville cases, used together, provide a very effective contrast that illuminates a number of aspects of power. While events took place in the 1970s, such basic political issues do not change over time. So, instructors should not be afraid to use these cases for fear they are old fashioned. Similarly, while the context is specific to the UK health care system, the structures, interest groups, and political dynamics are relevant to many other organizational and national settings.

The two cases show how a diverse political arena can be managed (and mismanaged). It is important to note that both the leading protagonists — the Area Management Team and the Community Health Council — lack the power to enforce a decision one way or the other. The most either can do is to persuade the Area Health Authority and the Secretary of State to support them and that, in turn, means influencing other interest groups and building coalitions. This requires the management of legitimacy and meaning. In Midville, managers successfully legitimized the closure; at Northville, opposition groups successfully 'delegitimized' it. Management of meaning hinges on symbolic power, which is differentially distributed — opposition groups at Northville had more than their counterparts at Midville, due to structural factors (such as the emotional appeal of the hospital, deprivation etc). The symbols that help create legitimacy vary from context to context. For example, financial arguments were persuasive at Midville but not at Northville, even though both Areas had deficits. Success ultimately depends on how well this power is mobilized — Northville managers were far less effective in this than Midville managers.

Northville management failed to close Park Road Maternity Hospital because they failed to convince anybody else — the employees, unions, Community Health Council, public or Area Health Authority — that the decision was justified, even though they had a commitment to the general principle of reducing the number of maternity beds in the city. The reasons for this are the following.

Management failed to use medical reasoning effectively. Their attempt to use the medical policy of locating maternity beds was countered by the fact that the doctors themselves contested the closure on medical grounds. They argued that a specialist hospital was *more* effective because it was devoted to high quality maternity care. Medical reasons are, as one would expect, a powerful influence in the health service since it is difficult for the public and lay members of the Area Health Authority to challenge them. Medical reasoning is also difficult to evaluate. For example, the policy of large integrated hospitals calling for 1,500 bed hospitals, advocated in the 1962 *Hospital Plan* and the 1967 *Bonham Carter Report*, was reversed in the 1980s in favour of small community hospitals. It is, therefore, very difficult to judge medical arguments objectively — what is often perceived as medically correct are those actions publicly supported by doctors, not those advocated by non-medical administrators.

Managers tried to present financial motives for the closure, arguing that the closure would save an estimated £550,000 per annum more than the alternative of closing maternity wards in other hospitals. The financial arguments were not accepted as legitimate justification for the reduction of services. The 1977 protest against cutbacks had been organized, despite the fact that the financial restrictions had been forced on management. The high unemployment, urban decline, poverty, and inadequate primary care in Northville seemed to rule out service cuts on the basis of finance alone.

Management failed to anticipate the emotional appeal of the hospital — its age, its longstanding position in the community, its survival of the Blitz, its devotion to maternity services, its production of appealing new-born babies, etc. Such factors led to public support for the fight against the closure which, in turn, led to the support of the media and local councillors. The interest of the latter in vote-winning local causes was high because of the balance of power in the council. The proposal to retain Park Road was, in fact, proposed and seconded by councillors. Management also failed to 'divide and conquer' the opposition by playing off Park Road supporters against those affected by the closure of the wards at Sackville and King Street hospitals.

The inability to use either medical or financial arguments to justify the closure meant that management was unable to legitimize its proposal. Had the Area Health Authority voted to proceed with the closure, the Community Health Council would probably have registered a formal protest and sent the final decision up to the Secretary of State. Union members would have threatened an occupation had there been no reprieve, which might have motivated the Secretary of State to revoke the closure, particularly since the recent protest had already forced him to set up a committee of inquiry.

Northville Area Health Authority (B)

The Park Road Action Committee immediately tried to build a coalition to fight the closure. They wrote to doctors, lobbied politicians, appeared on television and radio, spoke at a local Trades Council meeting, arranged public meetings, contacted the press and presented the Area Health Authority with a petition of more than 10,000 signatures opposing the closure. As a result, local media coverage was extensive. A television programme was aired in May 1977 which sided with the opponents of the closure. Local newspapers also tended to support the opponents. The Action Committee and Community Health Council expressed indignation at the low turnout for the Area Health Authority meeting. They claimed there had been gross under-representation with only a few of the 26 Area Health Authority members present at the Special Meeting, and they were angry that only nine took part in the vote.

Vocal doctors also began to question the closure. A letter from one of the consultant obstetricians at Park Road argued that the hospital should be retained precisely because it was such a good specialist hospital. This individual emerged as a public figure and appeared in several press articles, on TV and at public meetings. His opinion was reinforced by other medical personnel. A new consultant on the Area Health Authority remarked: 'If you close a hospital you can't re-open it, so you are losing options, but if you close wards you can always re-open them.' A professor of surgery, also an Area Health Authority member, was quoted in the press as saying that he was worried that the staff would be unable to cope if Park Road patients were transferred to King Street. Medical opinion thus appeared to be unanimous in its support for the retention of Park Road which made it difficult, if not impossible, for management to use medical justifications successfully in its proposal to close Park Road.

The Community Health Council continued to oppose the closure which meant that, should the Area Health Authority vote in favour of the proposal, the matter would probably be passed up to the ministerial level for a final decision.

In August 1977, another meeting of the Area Health Authority was held. Only 14 members attended, but 13 voted and the decision was 9 to 4 in favour of retaining Park Road and closing wards at King Street and Sackville General hospitals instead. By July 1978, the unions had agreed to the closure of these wards — the maternity wards at Sackville General Hospital closed in August

1978, and those at King Street General Hospital closed in September of the same year.

Questions

- Explain the reasons that account for management's failure to close Park Road Maternity Hospital.
- What are the ethical considerations concerning the actions of the various interest groups?

Midville Area Health Authority

Midville presents a very different picture. Managers were successful in closing Withybrooke Hospital because they provided mechanisms, such as compensation and consultation, to help employees deal with the change. They were also successful because they adopted a political approach that took into account *all* interest groups, including the Area Health Authority, the Community Health Council, the public and the government. Dale's view was that by being prepared for opposition, he was in a better position to deal with it. His aim was to: (a) assess the extent and nature of opposition; (b) to assess whether opposition would spread further than the local resistance to be expected in a hospital closure; and (c) if so, what were the implications and how powerful would the opponents be. Dale handled the closure in such a way as to minimize the chances of confrontation. As a result, the likelihood of government support was maximized. To further increase the chances of approval, the chairman took the battle over personally. He met with the relevant ministers in both governments and used his political skills to convince them of the need for closure.

This strategy was part of a long-term approach to industrial relations. Over time, management had built up credibility in the eyes of the unions, the Community Health Council and the public. Northville managers' previous disregard for consultation had created a negative image in the eyes of these groups. So, whereas Northville's management style compounded adversarial relations, Midville's style nurtured collaboration.

Another advantage for Midville managers was the fact that Withybrooke had none of the emotional appeal of Park Road. Also, the financial argument was easy to demonstrate to the potential opposition groups who were already well aware that the Area was grossly underfunded. The closure was accepted as a means of saving desperately needed cash. Financial criteria were more legitimate in this rural and relatively affluent area than in Northville. The rationalization argument, on the other hand, might have been less successful in convincing people of the need to close since there were conflicting medical opinions regarding the benefits of large integrated hospitals. Moreover, management was able to blame the financial exigency totally on the government whereas, in Northville, the deficit was blamed on previous mishandling of service cuts and other matters by Northville managers. Midville managers thus justified the closure far more effectively than their Northville counterparts.

These factors translated into a distribution of power that placed opposition groups at Midville in a far weaker position than their counterparts at Northville: they had none of the symbolic advantages and were relatively weak in the event of a strike or occupation. What is interesting to note is that Midville managers chose to adopt a strategy to legitimate the closure even though they had far more power to enforce a decision, as part of a long-term approach to industrial relations. Northville managers had little power to enforce a decision and failed to manage meaning and, subsequently, failed to close the hospital.

Midville Area Health Authority (B)

Management was well aware that the Community Health Council would probably send the decision up to the Secretary of State. Its strategy was, therefore, to reduce the chances of a united front opposing the closure which could force the government to overturn the closure decision.

> I thought that there was a good chance of this closure being accepted by the minister. The case was well made out, the local opposition was understandable and there was no real threat of the union behaving in such a way that would embarrass the government. In other words, I couldn't see it becoming a conflagration. I could see it being a difficulty which someone had to grasp. (Chairman)

This strategy thus hinged on consultation with the unions, the public and the employees, and on the provision of new wards for the doctors, which removed any medical objections to the closure.

The key figure was the chairman of the Area Health Authority — Alan Dale. He led many of the discussions, making himself available for consultation with all of the various interest groups. He was able to draw on his experience not only with the health service, with which he had been involved for 25 years, but with the local council. When he took the Area Health Authority chair in 1974, he was a member of the local council and so was able to capitalize on both his standing as a public figure and his political contacts. He was also in a position to apply the lessons he had learnt from the previous three closures undertaken by the Area Health Authority.

Dale's doctrine was to 'go and meet the people: people are compromised by the personal approach'. This he did by attending the public meeting, called in November 1977, to explain the reasons behind the closure. Consultation with the unions and the Community Health Council was also extensive. Employees were told personally, before they read about the proposed closure in the newspapers. Dale's strategy was supported by administrators, who were also convinced of the need for consultative management.

Another part of management's strategy involved emphasizing the necessity of the closure in the light of the financial position. The closure was presented as a financial imperative, even though there were other reasons why it took place.

I know darn well that had we had the money we still would have closed it. They (the unions and the Community Health Council) don't realize that. We were using the financial argument but what we were really after was rationalization. (Manager)

At Midville, the financial arguments were more acceptable to both the Area Health Authority and the public. Midville's precarious financial situation was attributed to external factors and its obligation to cater for patients outside the Area, unlike Northville where it was attributed to mismanagement. In the absence of an improvement in government funding, many people felt that there was no choice but to cut and reorganize services.

Management also offered employees a choice between layoff with compensation or redeployment in a comparable job where efforts were made to ensure that working conditions, shifts, hours etc. were the same as those at Withybrooke.

In December 1977, the Area Health Authority reaffirmed the decision to proceed with the closure but, because of the Community Health Council's action, passed the matter up to the Regional Health Authority. The Regional Health Authority also gave their support to the closure and passed the matter up again to the DHSS. In March 1979, the Secretary of State accepted the closure. The matter, however, was not finished. The new government, elected in May 1979, reserved the right to reconsider the closure. It was not until September 1979 that approval was finally given.

Questions

- Why was management successful at Midville and unsuccessful at Northville?
- What ethical issues should be considered in these cases?

Medical Services and Products Ltd

MSP is a complex case that is best used towards the end of the course when students have mastered the different aspects of power and can make feasible recommendations. It can also be used as a role-play, with students adopting the roles of the chief protagonists.

The class can commence with an analysis of the key players and their power. Much of Roberta's power — her expertise, credibility, information, board support, position, etc — depends on a successful move into biotechnology. Such a move is, however, a direct challenge to Donald who has considerable sources of power: position, information, experience, credibility, track record, expertise, political access to both the board and managers, charisma, and budgetary responsibility. The discussion can then focus on whether Roberta should fire Donald and, if so, the disadvantages of doing so. Students should be pushed into coming up with a comprehensive plan of action. Any plan has to address the issues of how to legitimate the move into biotechnology, gain control of the processes, and exploit resource power (see Hardy, C. and Redivo, F., 'Power and Organizational Development: A Framework for Change', *Journal of General Management*, forthcoming). The following case describes what actually happened.

Medical Services and Products Ltd (B)

Roberta knew she could not act unilaterally to fire or depose Donald. His power was too secure for that, and she would alienate key directors in any overt move to curtail his influence. She decided to bring in an external consultant to advise MSP on an appropriate structure and strategy. She chose a man who was a physicist by training. Roberta had considered a biotechnologist but decided that it would be redundant in the light of her own expertise, and would probably alienate Donald. The consultant — Bob Wheeler — carried out interviews with all vice-presidents and directors, professional and nonprofessional. He also maintained close contact with Roberta. From his interviews, Bob produced a series of tentative recommendations that he first cleared with Roberta. Following her approval, he produced a preliminary report that was circulated to the vice-presidents and directors who subsequently submitted a written response. Bob then carried out a series of individual and group meetings with them and produced a final report. This process took six months.

Roberta was reluctant to take action until the report was finalized; on the other hand, she did not want individuals to think that she was wasting time. She decided to tackle the low morale of the nonprofessional staff by conducting a series of informal group meetings. During these meetings, she discussed her vision for the company, tried to explain the potential that existed in the various scientific fields, and impress upon them how important they were to this effort. She made it clear she was open to their suggestions. She also made drop-in calls on professional and non-professional employees to get to know the company and its employees better. She resisted lobbying directors for fear of antagonizing them. She also spent a considerable amount of time collecting information and generally heightening the profile of her office.

She impressed upon board members the need to take the time necessary to produce a sound cultural and strategic change. She knew that the strength of their support would buy her some time, but she was also aware that her 'honeymoon' period was limited. If she could not demonstrate some achievement in the first 18 months, her days at MSP were probably numbered. To offset any feelings that she was not acting decisively enough internally, she used the time to build up external contacts and to form a basis for joint ventures, alliances, consulting expertise, and recruitment that would be needed in the future. Her research record and university experience helped her make some useful contacts and allowed her to provide the board with evidence that her time was being well spent.

Finally, Bob Wheeler's report was ready. It recommended that both Colin and Donald be moved. Colin had seen the writing on the wall and was not expected to offer much resistance. Roberta, however, did not want to create the picture that he had been heartlessly kicked out and offered him the post of special consultant for nonprofessional staff development. Donald was a trickier proposition. The report recommended that a special subsidiary be created to manage the external relationships resulting from product development (joint ventures, technology transfer, external contracts, etc), and that Donald should be put in charge of it. Donald's expertise made him the ideal candidate and the move had the added advantage of keeping him away from the centre stage. If he succeeded, the company would benefit. If his abrasive style alienated potential alliances, his failure would soon be visible and, more importantly, would be his alone.

The move had been partly legitimated by Bob Wheeler's study, but Roberta still had to use her talents to ensure that the directors and vice-presidents would not oppose her. The latter were less of a risk — there might be some promotion opportunities for them and they were close enough to the board to realize that Roberta had considerable support. Regardless of their loyalty to Donald, they were unlikely to want to go down with a sinking ship. The directors were more of a problem: they had strong personal loyalties to Donald who had welcomed them into the strategic decision making apparatus of the organization; they stood to lose the patronage they had derived from Donald's support; and some of them would be threatened by a reorientation towards biotechnology. If Roberta failed to secure their support or, at least, acquiescence for Donald's move, she would lose her authority and credibility. Moreover, a revolt or exodus of these people would put the strategic viability of the company in jeopardy.

Bob Wheeler's report supplied the reasons behind the change. When the final version was released, Roberta convened a meeting of the professional directors alone (she also had other meetings with the nonprofessional directors and the vice-presidents). While not overly antagonistic, they were fearful that they would not be able to function effectively without Donald's leadership. Roberta asked them to consider carefully if they wanted to resign over the issue. She reconvened the group two weeks later — without any resignations. In the intervening period, she had decided against lobbying individual directors, in case any perceptions of overt politics had an adverse effect.

Searches were conducted externally for replacements for Donald and Colin, though the individuals finally chosen were internal. It had the double advantage of demonstrating that the internal candidates were every bit as good as outsiders, and it opened up some promotion opportunities. A respected, professional director was selected to fill Colin's position. Roberta felt that it would add status to the nonprofessional functions if this senior position was acceptable to and accepted by the professional company elite. The Vice-president (Research) replaced Donald — since she had been a strong ally of Donald's, this promotion invalidated any accusation that Roberta was carrying out a vendetta. The Director of the Biotechnology Research team then became Vice-president (Research). In this way, Roberta felt that both biotechnology and traditional disciplines were represented at senior levels, and biotechnology could be more effectively incorporated into the research development of MSP.

Roberta also took over the key committees. She took the chair of the Management Advisory Committee (to which the Senior Vice-president (Finance and Administration) was added as an observer) and the Strategic Action Group (to which the Senior Vice-president (Finance and Administration) was added as a full member). The new Senior Vice-president (Development) continued to chair the Directors' Committee, while the Senior Vice-president (Finance and Administration) established an equivalent committee for the nonprofessionals. Once every three months, the committees would meet together, chaired by Roberta. In order to discuss all these changes, Roberta organized a retreat for all vice-presidents and directors.

Questions

- What is your opinion of Roberta's actions?
- Would you have done anything differently?

The Tobacco Firms

The tobacco firms can be used to illustrate the use of political strategies in an interorganizational arena and/or the ethical issues associated with the use of politics by dominant players to defend the status quo. I find it useful to divide the discussion into three parts: the analysis of the actions of the tobacco firms; recommendations for the anti-smoking lobby; a discussion of the ethical implications.

An analysis of the actions of the Big Six shows how sophisticated and complex their actions were. Since students often gloss over this fact, it is helpful to go through a fairly systematic analysis which includes clarifying the chronology of events, and identifying the players and their interests (see Tables 1, 2 and 3), before discussing the strategies. Once students are clear on how the tobacco firms successfully defended their domain, they can be pushed to come up with ideas for the anti-smoking lobby through to the present day, and to discuss the responses of the tobacco firms to this increasing encroachment. In this way, the case can be brought up to date.

A particularly revealing exercise is to require students to conduct research on the recent actions of the tobacco firms. These events are sufficiently well documented in the business literature to show that, in spite of the growing power of the anti-smoking lobby, the tobacco firms continue to defend their domain. They may have lost some battles (such as warning labels, advertising bans), but they are still winning the war: tobacco has yet to be regulated as a dangerous drug by the Federal Drug Administration (FDA) and the tobacco firms continue to reap considerable profits from the sale of tobacco products. These issues usually make for a spirited discussion of the ethical issues.

The tobacco firms used three basic strategies: information control; lobbying and coalition building; and advertising. All three served to defend the existing domain of the tobacco firms and to provide time to develop new tobacco products and overseas markets (domain offence) and diversify (domain creation). For example, Philip Morris bought 7-Up (soft drinks) in 1978, and Miller (beer) and Kraft (food products) in 1988.

Most of this material is taken from: R. Miles, *Coffin Nails & Corporate Strategies*, Englewood Cliffs NJ: Prentice Hall, 1982.

Table 1 *The events, 1950-1980*

Pre-1953	Scattered reports on health/smoking link Research on quality/yield No mention of health issues in annual reports
1953	Sloan Kettering Report
1954	Health statements in annual reports Increased in-house research and funding for 'independent' research Council for Tobacco Research founded
1958	Tobacco Institute (lobbying organization) founded
1963	FTC proposes advertising restrictions and health warnings $10 million given to AMA by tobacco firms
1964	Surgeon General's Report FTC holds hearings (Big Six do not appear) Clements becomes head of Tobacco Institute National Association of Broadcasters entertains 400+ of 535 members of Congress at its annual convention Cigarette Advertising Code proposed one month after FTC hearings — voluntary health warning but only on packs not on advertisements
1965	Funding for the Tobacco Research Council increases Congress overrules FTC: Cigarette Labelling and Advertising Act includes health warning but eliminates FTC's rule making power for 4 years (later 6 years) and prohibits other federal agencies from taking action on health warnings
1966	FTC sets up a cigarette tar and nicotine laboratory and makes a series of critical reports to Congress
1967	FTC attacks advertising of Big Six Advertising outlays of tobacco firms exceed $300 million
1968	FTC recommends advertising ban Fairness Doctrine provides equal air time to anti-smoking lobby Big Six stop mentioning TV sponsorship in annual reports Cost benefits of advertising ban acknowledged by Big Six Subpoenas issued on behalf of FTC for information on advertising (goes into litigation) Moss (anti-smoking) becomes chair of Senate Commerce Committee
1970	Voluntary ban on TV and radio advertising
1970-4	Big six derive benefits from ban
1973	$48 million given to 'independent' research by tobacco firms
1975	Grants to AMA total $18 million
1977	Judge rules against Big Six requiring detailed advertising information. Big Six appeal.

Table 2 *The smoking lobby*

The Big Six tobacco firms: smoking revenues total $7 billion in 1963
        Tobacco Tax Council
        Tobacco Institute
        Tobacco Research Council
Congress
        Federal, state, and municipal taxes total $3.25 billion
        26 states each earn more than $100 million in tobacco taxes
        Representatives from the six tobacco states chair one quarter of congressional committees, including the Senate Commerce Committee

Advertising/Media groups
        National Association of Broadcasters
        Tobacco firms total $300 million in advertising outlays
        One third members of Congress owned major stockholdings in radio and TV

Farmers
        One acre of tobacco raises rent of $1,000 vs $100 for soybeans

Workers, unions
        34,000 workers work in manufacturing plants alone
        600,000 families in 26 states dependent on tobacco as primary income source

Table 3 *The anti-smoking lobby*

American Medical Association: its opposition came relatively late in the day — it did not vote for a ban on cigarette advertising until 1985. Critics have suggested that the generosity of the tobacco firms led to its silence during the FTC hearings.

Department of Health, Education and Welfare.

Federal Trade Commission (FTC): regulates advertising

Federal Communications Commission (FCC)

Various anti-smoking groups such as heart and cancer institutes.

Information

This strategy was carried out by conducting research, individually and jointly, by the tobacco firms specifically in response to the health threat. Before 1953, there had been no research undertaken by the Big Six on health issues.

Following the 1953 Sloan Kettering Report, health statements started to appear in annual reports; in-house research on health was created; the Council for Tobacco Research was founded; and 'independent' research was funded. This impetus increased further after the 1964 Surgeon General's Report.

The benefits of this strategy are considerable: the Big Six are the 'first to know'; they can suppress adverse information and filter information, thereby controlling the supply of information to the FTC and Congress; it creates a dependency of researchers on the tobacco firms and helps to coopt 'independent' researchers and the AMA; it forces the anti-smoking lobby to do research which takes time and money, and reduces their credibility in the meantime; it buys the tobacco firms a lead time; and it creates legitimacy for the tobacco firms as responsible corporate citizens.

Lobbying and Coalition Building

This strategy was carried out by the Tobacco Institute in response to the FTC attempt to legislate against the tobacco firms in 1963. The tobacco firms proposed the Cigarette Advertising Code (voluntary monitoring) which was passed by Congress. It had two main benefits. First, it changed the decision making arena from FTC to Congress: from an arena where the key players were largely independent of tobacco firms to one where numerous players were highly dependent on them through taxes, employment, advertising etc. These players were also powerful by virtue of their control of key committees and by force of numbers. Second, this strategy redefined the issue from health to 'democracy', which was difficult to vote against; made unity easier to secure; cut across party lines; coopted neutral parties; and led to circumscribed FTC powers.

At this point, the FTC was out of action, and the anti-smoking lobby was split, politically inexperienced, had no money and was lagging in research. The FTC started to disseminate information, carry out research, form coalitions and create unity. It was helped by the Fairness Doctrine.

The Advertising Strategy

The gradual accumulation of power by the anti-smoking lobby eventually led to an advertising ban, but it was delayed until 1970 by the strategies of the tobacco firms. Moreover, the Big Six were not only prepared for it but were able to recoup significant cost savings, through their experience in European markets and the voiding of the Fairness Doctrine.

Update

At the time of the case, the anti-smoking lobby was weak, disunited, under-resourced, and lacked expertise and information. Gradually, their access to power sources such as information, political access and lobbying expertise has grown. Also new groups entered the coalition, including airlines that have banned smoking on flights, municipalities which have drawn up local legislation banning smoking; insurance companies that have offered reduced rates for nonsmokers; and lawyers who have become involved in litigation against the tobacco firms. Also, over time, the evidence demonstrating a link between smoking and health problems has increased, with the effects of secondary smoking now being a major cause for concern. Moreover, environmental and health concerns have been placed higher on the societal agenda and have served to discredit smoking further.

Despite these changes, tobacco firms have remained highly profitable. Philip Morris made $3 billion in profit in 1992, most of which came from tobacco products with margins of over 40 per cent. R.J. Reynolds made $2.3 billion from tobacco profits in 1991. The tobacco firms were the best performing group in the stock market during the 1980s and returned over 1,500 per cent over the decade (*Barrons*, 8-26, 9 July 1990). In the USA, the industry employs 710,000 individuals and generates $60 billion of GNP. Tobacco products account for $13 billion in taxation and over $3 billion in advertising (*Report on Business*, p. 25, September 1987).

The tobacco firms have been criticized for targeting vulnerable groups such as developing countries and, in the domestic market, young girls and minorities. One economist has been quoted as saying that poorer people make better targets because they have 'less of an investment in the future. If you're a black male living in the ghetto, your principal health priority to age 45 is going to be avoiding homicide. It may not be very interesting that you're going to gain 7 years at the end of your lifespan if you don't smoke' (*Report on Business*, p. 26, September 1987). Brown and Williamson's advertising consultant recommended targeting young females and presenting cigarettes as an initiation to the adult world like other illicit activities such as sex and drugs (*Report on Business*, p. 24, September 1987), though he was later dismissed by the company. There have been criticisms that children have been targeted — a US government report estimated that 80 per cent of smokers are addicted by the age of eighteen. R.J. Reynolds has come under particular scrutiny for its marketing campaign for Camel cigarettes using a cartoon character. A 1992 report by the American Medical Association reported that 'Old Joe Camel' was connected to cigarettes by children as young as three years. Camel's share of the under-age market had increased from one-half of one per cent to 33 per cent as a result of the advertising campaign (*Business Week*, p. 34, 23 December 1991). Part of the promotional campaign involved redeeming 3 empty Camel packs for a Joe Camel T-shirt, or 140 packs for a leather jacket (by which time the consumer would almost certainly be addicted!).

Estimates suggest that over 350,000 Americans and 2.5 million individuals worldwide die each year from smoking-related diseases. The US health care costs of smoking were estimated in a government report to be $52 billion in 1990. The tobacco firms have continued to deny that the link between smoking and health is conclusive.

PART III MANAGING STRATEGIC PREDICAMENTS

Introduction

This part tackles a number of specific predicaments or contemporary strategic challenges. It can be used in conjunction with material from the other two parts as a component of courses on strategic change or politics. Nearly all these cases can be approached from both a 'strategic' and a 'political' viewpoint.

Mergers and acquisitions are, obviously, a key strategic challenge that a large number of firms have had to deal with. There are also major political ramifications that may occur during the merger itself (such as RJR/Nabisco) or afterwards. Melding two power structures and two cultures is by no means easy, as Fulmer and Gilkey show. GM/EDS provides an interesting example of how a merger of two disparate cultures was eventually successful. Machiavelli's *The Prince* makes for an interesting accompaniment for instructors who wish to flesh out the political issues. Declining resources make management even more of a zero-sum game. In addition to the strategic issues, politics is a key feature of managing decline because of possibilities of resistance. The Hardy chapter and the AECL case show how resistance can be minimized.

Innovation is a key strategic challenge for managers, and it is also a political challenge because of the difficulties in transcending disciplinary boundaries and the uncertainty of innovation. Because innovation can not be 'measured', it may be difficult to predict how much to invest and in which projects. Employees and managers tend to push their particular project to ensure it is funded. Dougherty discusses some of the theory behind successful innovation in her chapter, and some of the practical realities are reviewed in the Machco case. The global environment adds considerable complexity to strategy making because of the cultural and geographic factors involved in tackling global markets in today's business world. The Wortzel chapter clarifies some of the issues involved in formulating a global strategy, which students can apply to the case on the Bicycle Components Industry.

Sustainable development has only recently become a strategic issue for many companies, and it brings them directly into conflict with a lot of environmental activists. The Loblaws case shows the political difficulties encountered as business meets activist, and the role of bridging organizations. Finally, managing consensus would appear to be devoid of political issues but, as the Conglom case and Westley's chapter demonstrate, allowing middle management to participate in the strategy making process and making it inclusive rather than exclusive can be intensely political.

PART III CASES

General Motors and Electronic Data Systems

GM's acquisition of EDS can be used to explore a number of issues. First, it can be discussed at the strategic level. Did the acquisition make strategic sense? Many students will think it was a mistake and that the EDS culture will be swallowed up by GM. To address this issue, instructors may have to elaborate on the potential offered to both companies by outsourcing GM's information systems. It is worthwhile to take students through this process step by step. Outsourcing means that EDS becomes responsible for *all* of GM's data processing operations. It represents an enormous opportunity for growth for EDS and the opportunity to save money and improve services for GM. However, EDS lacks the necessary expertise to achieve this single-handedly. So, a large proportion of the 9,000 GM transferees will be needed in EDS to provide this expertise, even though they represent a possible dilution of EDS culture. Outsourcing companies continually struggle with this challenge — every time they sign a contract they may be dramatically increasing their size by taking in people from another company with a vastly different culture.

A second issue follows from the first. The strategic potential of the acquisition can be realized only if two key issues are successfully managed: the independence of EDS vis-à-vis GM so that the former's strengths are not compromised; and the integration of EDS and GM data processing personnel. The challenges associated with mergers and acqusitions are thus compounded in the case of outsourcing because people from both companies have to be successfully integrated: the option of keeping both companies totally separate is not feasible. The challenge of integration draws students' attention to the specific, operational issues that must be resolved: benefits, compensation, contracts, unions, new hires, etc. In addition, students should consider how EDS can be structured to deal with this massive growth. If students are pushed, they will realize the enormity and diversity of GM's computer systems. They range from CAD-CAM in design, to administrative records, to health benefits, to process technology on the shop floor, to warranty and sales information in the dealerships. Once the diversity and magnitude of this task is realized, the need for some form of divisionalization, as discussed in the B case, becomes clear. In addition, some consideration should be given to a structure that will facilitate the exploration of business outside of GM. (By 1993, EDS' dependence on GM had been reduced from three-quarters to one half of its business.)

Finally, the case can be used to review some of the basic concepts associated with the management of strategic change discussed in the first part of the book: culture, structure, leadership styles, reward systems, growth of an entrepreneurial company, etc. Of particular interest is the contrast in the leadership styles of Perot and Smith. Students may be familiar with Perot following his presidential campaign in 1992 and Smith's style comes under close scrutiny in the film *Roger and Me*.

General Motors and Electronic Data Systems (B)

In 1986, a faction of the Board attempted to make Perot tone down his criticisms. Since he owned $11.3 million in shares, he was by far the company's largest shareholder: trying to freeze out Perot was compared to scuttling part of GM itself. Nevertheless, in December 1986, GM paid $700 million to buy out Perot and three other senior executives from EDS including the President (Meyerson), who was credited with managing the company's growth in the 1970s. Perot lost his seat on the board, agreed not to set up a profit-making competitor for three years, and risked fines of $7.5 million for publicly criticizing GM. The other executives were also prevented from setting up in competition with EDS. The deal was worth twice the market value of the shares, which had fallen sharply during the latter half of 1986. Before he left, Perot negotiated the continuation of EDS's independence, a commitment by GM to supply EDS with long-term contracts, and to allow bonus stock awards to be cashed in after 13 months instead of the usual 5-10 years. Lester M. Alberthal replaced Perot as head of EDS, but no longer reported directly to Smith. EDS became part of a subsidiary that included Hughes Aircraft and Delco Electronics.

The focal point of the integration between GM's data processing personnel and EDS was an operation in Detroit, headed by Senior Vice-president Kenneth G. Riedlinger — a one-time catholic missionary. He set up a new integrated operation and assigned five former GM executives and ten EDS managers to run the 15 data processing divisions. 1,000 EDS and 1,200 new hires (from outside both EDS and GM) were brought in to streamline GM's computer operations. They ran into considerable resistance in GM plants where engineers employed their non-IBM compatible equipment to prevent EDS personnel from gaining access to their territory. GM employees resented EDS personnel invading their company with the notion that they were white knights on a mission of mercy. It seemed to them that EDS had taken over GM rather than the other way around, especially when Perot continued to speak of EDS as 'his' company. There were also problems with some 9,000 resentful employees who had been transferred to EDS from GM. EDS agreed to pay their old (GM) wages and grant them $15,000 worth of the new class E shares, but they had to give up overtime pay, accept less generous benefits and lose job tenure. They were particularly resentful about the loss of GM's pension plan that allowed retirement after 30 years' service, and launched union challenges at 14 of the 200 GM data processing sites taken over by EDS. Riedlinger wrote a letter criticizing the union organizing drive as 'the work of a small number of people (who) are disgruntled and apparently motivated by an intention to get even with GM' (quoted in *Business Week*, 11 February 1983, p. 119), which only fuelled the antagonisms. GM then stepped in with a new offer: early retirement to workers with a specified amount of seniority, or severance packages as an alternative to transfer. Six hundred (10 per cent of those eligible) accepted. Many of those who did not leave remained unhappy about being moved to a company whose code of ethics resembled a 'nineteenth century, presbyterian hymn book' (quoted in *Business Week*, 7 April 1986, p. 84).

Seventy per cent of EDS's business came from GM after the acquisition, but fights continued over the contracts. GM insisted on cost-plus contracts, leaving EDS with margins of only 9.5 per cent as opposed to the 14 per cent it obtained from its outside work. EDS profit margins suffered as a result, falling from 8.5 per cent in 1984 to 5.5 per cent in 1985 (and were still only at 8 per cent in 1988). With cost-plus contracts (and widely held E shares), it was in the interests of EDS to hire as many people as possible and charge high prices: a strategy that did little to forge a team spirit between the two companies. These frictions slowed the restructuring and factory automation. EDS also overestimated the sophistication of users, especially dealers, and failed to provide adequate training or accurately predict the costs of learning the new systems.

Despite these problems, EDS's revenues escalated from less than $1 billion in 1984 to over $6 billion in 1990 (Table 1), thanks largely to its captive market at GM, although GM continued to run into problems (Table 2). EDS employees numbered over 48,000. EDS installed the largest private telecommunications system in the world for GM, in only three years instead of the expected ten. Some of its least glamorous projects were the most cost-effective. EDS saved GM $750 million in health care benefits between 1984 and 1988. Its ability to simplify projects often produced savings. For example, a project at one of GM's plants to install a ten-year computerized history of all engines built at the plant was reduced to a six-month history with considerable savings and no loss in effectiveness. The size of EDS translated into formidable discounts from suppliers. It became the largest buyer of IBM mainframes. A joint project with Hitachi to buy National Advanced Systems, which manufactured IBM-compatible mainframes, provided EDS with direct access to equipment, as well as leverage over IBM in systems integration.

EDS was initially less effective with its business outside GM. While it was able to install a $500 million telecommunications system at GM, its three-year old telecommunications division had revenues of only $100 million in 1988, and an attempt to get a large contract from the federal government for its phone system failed. Its factory automation business outside GM was also limited.

Table 1 *EDS financial performance, 1985-1992*

	Revenue ($ billion)	Profit ($ billion)
1985	3.5	.20
1986	4.4	.26
1987	4.4	.32
1988	4.8	.38
1989	5.5	.44
1990	6.1	.50
1991	7.1	.55
1992	8.2	.64

Source: 1985-87: *Moody's*, 1988, Vol. 1
1988-90: *Moody's*, 1991, Vol. 1
1991-92: *Moody's*, 1993, Vol. 1

Table 2 *GM financial performance, 1985-1992*

	Revenue ($ billion)	Profit ($ billion)
1985	96.4	4.0
1986	102.8	2.9
1987	114.9	3.6
1988	123.6	4.8
1989	126.9	4.2
1990	124.7	(2.0)
1991	123.1	(4.5)
1992	132.4	(23.5)

Source: 1985-86: *Moody's*, 1988, Vol. 1
1987-92: *Moody's*, 1993, Vol. 1

Eventually, a cultural detente was declared between EDS and GM. EDS employees no longer had to wear suits and could sport beards at work. GM finally accepted fixed price contracts and, in 1988, 80 per cent of its contracts with EDS conformed to this principle as opposed to 9 per cent in 1984. The margins on these contracts increased to 13 per cent. GM also provided EDS with a $1 billion dollar loan (interest free and only $800 million repayable). EDS used this money to give low interest loans to customers as an advance on the expected savings on projects — giving rise to complaints that EDS was buying contracts.

In June 1988, Ross Perot set up Perot Systems — a new computer services company whose office overlooked EDS's Dallas headquarters. Since he was prohibited from setting up a profit-making enterprise for another year, he offered a contract to the US Postal Service at cost. A number of companies, including EDS, complained and the US Senate forced the withdrawal of the contract on the grounds that the project had not gone through the required bidding process. Nevertheless, Perot continued with his new company, and five of his first eight hires were EDS people. The following year, Perot recruited 50 EDS managers including eight from the most senior levels. He received 6,000 applications, including many from EDS employees. But it was in 1992 when Perot really hit the limelight -- by standing as an independent candidate for the US presidency!

Question

- Why was GM's acquisition of EDS successful?

Atomic Energy of Canada Ltd

AECL is a downsizing case where students can be asked to devise a retrenchment plan that takes into account the corporation's public and political responsibilities as well as its business needs. The students' plans can then be contrasted with the actions undertaken by AECL in case B, and students can be asked to consider some of the advantages and disadvantages of these particular actions, and how these actions related to the particular culture of the organization. While these events occurred following the recession in the early 1980s, it is obvious from events a decade later that downsizing remains a managerial challenge. As a result, the lessons of the 1980s are relevant today, particularly since AECL involves professional employees — while such employees bore a relatively small brunt of earlier recessions (estimates suggest less than 25 per cent of layoffs in the 1980s were of professional, white-collar workers), they are a large component (over 40 per cent) of contemporary layoffs.

Certainly, some aspects of the downsizing programme caused resentment. The first was the lack of planning, which had caused a sudden switch from hiring to downsizing leading to considerable frustration, particularly among the recently hired graduates. Managers admitted that this had been a tactical error that could damage their profile — and ability to hire — in the future. Another cause for concern was the selective nature of dismissals, especially when seniority was overruled. Managers admitted that the selection criteria of the Manpower Steering Committee were not always objective. Students often react against seniority as a criterion for hiring and firing, but it does serve to protect employees from subjective and unfair decisions. At AECL, some managers and most employees thought that seniority should have been used to avoid accusations of grudges and politics. Critics of selected dismissals also point out that dismissals for performance reasons should be kept separate from redundancies, otherwise employees who lose jobs through no fault of their own also have to deal with the stigma of poor performance. The very existence of 'deadwood' indicates that AECL had not been effective in supervising performance before the layoffs, probably as a result of the massive expansion in the 1970s, and it is questionable whether the retrenchment programme was the appropriate place to rectify poor managerial decisions.

A programme based on seniority could have been coupled with a voluntary or early retirement package that would have induced some of the older, longer serving employees to leave, freeing up jobs for younger employees. Such a scheme was made available at AECL, but only eight months after the enforced dismissals and with the same compensation package. Nonetheless, over 80 people took advantage of it. The president approved the voluntary package only when it was made clear that there would be no additional expenses. Had it been offered at the beginning of the cutbacks, however, it might have freed up jobs, projected an image of caring on to AECL, and avoided some of the problems caused by the selective dismissals. It might also have prevented the 120 grievances of which 24 led to reinstatement (19 out of 71 for unionized and 5 out of 49 for non-unionized grades).

Employees quickly became disenchanted with the Joint Planning Committee because management was unwilling to discuss alternative ways in which the downsizing could be accomplished. It was 'bolting the stable door after the horse had gone because the corporation had already made its decisions'. The unwillingness to explore alternatives to enforced dismissals confirmed opinions that management was not acting in good faith. The voluntary package, which emerged out of the Joint Planning Committee, was offered only after the majority of layoffs had been decided. Other alternatives, including worksharing (involving a temporary 10 per cent reduction in working hours), leave without pay, and active outplacement to other sites were 'completely rejected out of hand'. The Joint Manpower Adjustment Committees, on the other hand, met with employee approval because they provided a 'two way dialogue'. The outplacement and grievance subcommittees were also considered very effective. The two non-unionized groups were particularly appreciative of these subcommittees since non-unionized employees access to the same outplacement facilities and grievance procedures as their unionized counterparts.

The 16-week notice period met with mixed reviews. Some managers felt that: 'it took strong, determined managers to keep production up'. In general, however, it was seen as an effective and humane strategy. The outplacement programme was also considered a success. Of 26 terminated PSAC members, eight had been placed by 1 June 1983. Of 102 SPEA members, 56 found alternative employment. Some people, however, failed to make use of the available services. For example, for a seminar on interview techniques, 100 people were contacted, 40 expressed interest, 13 registered, but only four actually attended. These problems were sometimes attributed to the individuals concerned, by managers who saw them as 'their own worst enemies', but critics suggested that attendance would have been improved had the seminars been held during work time. For example, at the initial seminar, 98 per cent attendance was recorded, and 77 per cent of terminated employees attended the job fair.

The morale of some of the remaining employees was undoubtedly damaged by the retrenchment process. People were worried about the precarious position of the industry, and some were disenchanted with AECL. Other employees were more appreciative of the corporation's efforts. Ironically, the retrenchment programme provided an opportunity for the Human Resource department to demonstrate its worth through its management of the outplacement programme. A new Executive Vice-president with an engineering background was appointed as head of the Human Resource department. His credibility as an engineer had helped to improve the status of the function.

The total cost of the retrenchment programme worked out to nearly $4 million. It included settlements ranging from $2,000 to $40,000, the cost of the committees, seminars, grievances, and job searching and outplacement programmes. This exercise was only one of a number of downsizing initiatives undertaken by AECL during this period. Net income fell by 60 per cent between 1983 and 1984, but subsequently improved - net income in 1987 was 90 per cent higher than in 1984 (although it was still lower than in 1982). Employee numbers were down to 5,000 in 1987 — 38 per cent lower than in 1982 (see Table 1).

Table 1   *AECL performance, 1981-1989*

	1981	1982	1983	1984	1985	1986	1987	1988	1989
Total revenue ($ millions)	611	505	409	370	309	260	277	290	228
Operating profit ($ millions)	29	27	26	15	8	28	22	32	49
Net income ($ millions)	13	20	23	9	10	17	17	10	23
Number of employees	7512	7871	7327	6978	6767	5540	5007	4892	4274

Source: 1981-85: *1984/5 Annual Report*, p. 23
              1986-89: *1988/9 Annual Report*, p. 27

Atomic Energy of Canada Ltd (B)

Individuals were selected for redundancy on the basis of seniority: the 600 individuals with the least seniority would lose their jobs. Senior management decided to make allowances for critical skills: some employees with less seniority would retain their jobs if they had certain designated skills. Voluntary termination was rejected on the grounds of cost.

> A voluntary scheme would not have given us those numbers. If you make a package rich enough you would get the number that you want. Unfortunately we didn't feel, financially, it was appropriate. (Manager)

There was a fear of publicity and accusations of wasting taxpayers' money if an overly generous severance package was provided.

> As a crown corporation we do have political visibility. [It] was an incentive to be cautious about this process, to plan it carefully so it could stand up to close scrutiny - political and public. (Manager)

> One of the strongest constraints in our layoff was that we did not wish to be featured on the CBC, in the *Globe and Mail* or anywhere else. We succeeded — perhaps by being too conservative. (Manager)

Nor did line managers want to lose control over deciding who stayed and who left. Human resource managers supported voluntary severance but were unable to convince senior executives.

> If the Human Resource department had been more powerful and management had been less control oriented, alternatives might have been considered. (Joint Planning Committee member)

A Manpower Steering Committee was established in September 1982 to specify the critical skills. It was chaired by the Vice-president (Engineering) and consisted of other vice-presidents. Members believed that the exemption of those employees with necessary skills from layoff was vital to AECL's future.

> Had we laid off in strict seniority in unionized and non-unionized sectors, the corporation would collapse. We just [wouldn't have been able to] cope with the [skilled] people we would lose. (Manager)

Seniority was also unofficially circumvented to remove poor performers.

> One of my intentions was to use this as an opportunity to weed out deadwood. . . . When you have to retrench you really have to identify the non-performers regardless of what the rules are. (Manager)

The Manpower Steering Committee established a subcommittee to identify the exact individuals to be laid off. The aim was to inform the employees at the same time as the notice of group dismissals was given — to inform individuals as early as possible.

> If you had let it be known beforehand that you were laying off one quarter of the corporation, then you would have had the whole corporation worried rather than the specific quarter, and I think that would have had a tremendous effect on production. (Manager)

The subcommittee was, however, unable to produce 600 names, so the layoffs were broken down into two phases. The first occurred during February and March 1983, when the 510 individuals that had been identified would leave. The remaining individuals, as yet unidentified, were to leave later that year.

Another feature of the layoffs was the use of consultation committees. As required by law, a Joint Planning Committee was created to find a way of reducing or eliminating the need for dismissals. The corporation had, however, already decided on the principle of selected dismissals. Its view was that, while some form of discussion was valid, it should not involve the overall retrenchment plan.

> It wasn't in the interests of the employees to try to reverse the decision or try to get more compensation. The corporation has made these decisions and they are irrevocable, so let's try and get on with the business of finding jobs. (Manager)

> We were not prepared to negotiate the plan we had put together (because) the plan was a good one. To some extent we were not prepared to consult; we had decided what we were going to do and how we were going to do it. (Manager)

The corporation also established a Joint Manpower Adjustment Committee to deal with grievances and outplacement for each of the four employee groups. They had management and employee or union representation and met weekly from November 1982 to June 1983. Outplacement subcommittees were responsible for examining ways of helping redundant employees look for new jobs. Grievance subcommittees were used to resolve any grievances that arose from alleged transgressions of seniority by the corporation. Grievance procedures already existed for the unionized groups. Special procedures were introduced for the non-unionized groups which, previously, had not had access to them. In the latter case, procedures were not fully binding as in the case of union groups whose grievances would go before a formal arbitration process, but they did provide individuals with access to senior management.

The people who lost their jobs had access to outplacement aid. It included a two-day seminar on job searching techniques, after-hours instruction on interviewing techniques, and financial counselling. The Human Resource department helped employees by providing resumé preparation, reference letters, 'ad tracking', exploratory letters to potential employers, advertising, job posting, and personal counselling. A job fair was also arranged in which potential employers were invited to the site. AECL also provided severance pay: approximately one week's pay for each year of service (standard policy), plus an additional one-half day for each month of service for employees under age 45 and one day for those over age 45.

Questions

- What do you think of AECL's retrenchment plan?
- How do you think employees will react?

Machco's New Finishing Machine

This case focuses on a specific new product effort, and includes some insight into the organizational context necessary to sustain multiple innovation efforts. The discussion should begin with the Hurricane effort itself to develop some understanding of what a successful product innovation effort looks like, and then consider whether and how an established organization can change to accommodate more innovation *along with* routine products.

How did the Hurricane team incorporate market and customer needs into the product's design? What types of market-technology knowledge did they develop and fail to develop? Was the development process creative?

The case illustrates a fairly complete product concept development. The team was given a set of objectives up-front which framed their thinking. However, note that they needed to jointly visit customers in order to bring the product idea alive. This 'visceralization' process allowed the people to see the finishing tool in action, to appreciate how people used it, and to come to understand the important product features, such as its performance, its fit and ease of use. The engineer was surprised to find that customers were 'using it wrong,' which was an important insight for him — customers do not use a product 'wrong,' the product needs to be designed for use. Also, one might discuss the distributors' conservative perspectives on what the product should look like: it should be just like the competition's, not be strange in any way. Their ideas show the flaws of asking 'salespeople' to provide market specifications.

For feasibility: On the technology side, team members knew about product technology constraints but had to discover the composite material as the best way to deliver the shape. The manufacturing feasibility was not well addressed, since they could not make the shell. The market feasibility was fairly well covered. The team did not know for sure whether the product would actually sell until they put prototypes out, but their early work eliminated a good part of the uncertainty. In addition, the team realized that another me-too or copy cat product would not buy them enough market share. To succeed in this mature market, they had to come out with a demonstrably better product.

The trends they used included ergonomics for design, use of composites in manufacturing, and design for manufacturing/assembly (DFM, DFA). For the last, they did reduce the number of parts (DFA: the fewer parts, the easier to assemble), but they did not really use design for manufacturing, which is a technique to design a part for functionality and manufacturing at the same time. The engineer designed the shell without any manufacturing input.

Creativity: While the product was 'just' a redesign (not the first Xerox machine or jet engine), it had a number of creative elements. Challenge the students to identify them and sort out what enabled the team to be creative. The creative design was in part due to collaboration. Generally, no function has enough insight into the customer needs; the product concept emerges iteratively as a multifunctional team goes out and sees, and then puts together various ideas. Bringing in a fresh perspective from the design house helped, as did the models, to give the product possibilities a physical reality. Finally, the fact that the team was able to, and was allowed to, engage in frame-breaking thinking, like using composites, was important to creativity.

What organizing factors were critical to the Hurricane's apparent success? How were these processes different than the usual ones at Machco?

One essential organizing factor was the multidisciplinary team. Just having a team was not enough. The team *owned* the product concept development — they created the product idea themselves — and everyone felt responsible for the full product concept (except for the manufacturing part). Seeing the whole helped people see how their part fit in, so they no longer worked in abstract. The team also multiplied the 'manhours' since, as one person said, everyone would go out on the shop floor together to solve a problem. Other innovators have talked about how, because the team gave them the sense that everyone else was working hard, they would also work harder. The team's leadership was shared, which, while perhaps not essential to all teams, certainly helped here. The instructor can challenge the students to discuss team formation and leadership for innovation, and how it might be different from, say, a committee or work group doing routine work.

Another organizing factor was senior management's hands-off stance. They did not interfere, but supported the team and gave them the resources they needed. The students can discuss what senior management's role should be in innovation, and how should an innovation team relate to them?

A third factor was the 'suspension' of the scrap rule. Machco operated the plant on a standard cost system, in which the production of all parts is first 'standardized' and, then, anything over the standard is considered to be variance. Scrap is the ultimate sin, since it is all variance. This system emphasizes utilization of labour and equipment, under the premise that the more you maximize the use of machinery and labour the more you control costs. The system in effect punishes experimentation.

The discussion should recognize that all of these key organizing factors were unique to the Hurricane project, and different from usual.

Why did manufacturing drop the ball, or did they? What is the relationship between an innovation and the other functions and products?

The problems in manufacturing highlight the need to make more systematic changes to enable innovation. The manufacturing process is complex, especially if, like at Machco, hundreds of different models of scores of products are being produced. Simply adding innovations on to that complex (and tightly controlled via the standard cost system) process will become problematic. Moreover, simply having a person 'represent' manufacturing on the team will not assure that the new parts can be manufactured. The case indicates that fairly extensive changes were needed in manufacturing (for example, a whole new way of organizing, controlling the processes, and evaluating), but were not made. However, developing some pilot lines and beginning to train in DFM are change processes that could have helped.

Machco decided that the major flaw in their system was that the leadership role on the innovation team was not clearly defined. They changed the process to add a project manager who reported to the head of engineering. In 1990, Group managers started three new product efforts, all with the same one-year deadline. How do you suppose they performed? Why? Can you recommend any other changes at Machco to foster innovation?

All three products were way over budget and way over time. The new structure emphasized the design and engineering process to the exclusion of everything else. None of the new teams visited customers jointly, because they all felt that they already knew the customers. In two cases the marketing and engineering departments fought over the design, and marketing rejected the designs. All projects had serious manufacturing problems as well. Senior management got annoyed with all the problems and intervened directly in the projects, dictating solutions. This created even more turmoil, because the dictated solutions did not take into account certain issues the innovators were trying to deal with, and because they made the team members feel not responsible for decisions. Why? Because none of the organizing factors or market-technology knowledge development factors that were crucial to

Hurricane's success was institutionalized. The overall plant was expected to meet the volumes and schedules for all the current products. When push came to shove, the people reverted to Machco's usual system, which did not facilitate innovation.

Machco needs a strategy that indicates how innovations fit with current products. Such a strategy would include a manufacturing strategy to invest in new systems (that is, composites), and allow for experimentation. The strategy would also specify the kinds of products or markets that are a priority, so that not too much would be attempted at once. In addition, senior managers were very detached from the plant, and saw no conflict in asking people to innovate extensively and, at the same time, meet the current production schedule. These managers needed to connect with the reality of operations if the strategy was to work.

Some people feel that old firms cannot innovate, which is too bad since firms like Machco must do so to keep their products viable. The students can debate this issue: can Machco become truly innovative? How should they proceed to implement the new organizing processes to support innovation?

The Bicycle Components Industry

Groups or individuals can present their findings and recommendations to the class. For example, the class can be divided into two: one group proposing the future strategies to be taken by Shimano; the other could do the same for Campagnolo. The class in plenary can analyze the companies and their different strategies.

Each company has a distinct strategy: while Shimano pursued a mission to expand product range and segment coverage, Campagnolo was a niche player, concentrating exclusively on top of the range racing equipment. The founding fathers placed very different cultural blueprints on their respective organizations. Shozoburo was an engineer and businessman, driven by the need to succeed commercially, while Tullio was primarily a cyclist inspired by technical excellence and a desire to be recognized at the top of cycle racing.

Campagnolo has always been associated with competitive cycling since its founder was an amateur racer. His aim was to develop products specifically for the needs of the sports cyclist: a person primarily concerned with speed. It is therefore easy to see how Tullio saw a niche he could exploit. Japan, on the other hand, does not have the same racing tradition, and bicycles were a cheap, practical, low cost and low maintenance form of transport — very different to the Italian context. While there is very little competitive cycling in Japan, there is 'Keirin' track racing which is rather like greyhound racing, but with bikes instead of dogs. Shozoburo Shimano was instrumental in developing Keirin as a way of promoting sports cycling. The Japanese tend to use cycling for leisure and utility purposes, so Shimano found that riders were more concerned with comfort than speed. Shimano promoted the company as one that makes 'equipment for outdoor activities' rather than simply bicycle components. The two men were products of their environments, so appreciating the context of cycling in Italy and Japan is important.

The personalities and backgrounds of these key individuals, however, are only part of the overall set of factors in determining organizational structure and strategy. The class should also consider the succession strategies of these two companies in the light of the founders' original objectives. The formative years

---

of the two companies set the agenda in terms of their founders' views on quality. The case provides an opportunity to consider what is meant by quality in each of the firms.

Issues of new product development are also central. One of the ways in which Shimano took the industry by storm was with its innovation programme and commitment to R & D. Campagnolo lost the innovation initiative early in its history. This feeds back to the strategy of pursuing the racing market only, a strangely conservative fraternity where the mindset assumes that 'if it doesn't hurt, it isn't really cycling', and where new designs or products aimed at making things easier and more comfortable are almost frowned upon. Only time-saving innovations are welcomed. Shimano, on the other hand, was coming from a different position based upon the idea of easier biking.

Supply chain management is a further area for examination. Shimano had considerable power over its customers, causing resentment among OEMs (original equipment manufacturers). It is a good example of this particular problem and may be used to stimulate debate about whether and how Shimano might contain the resentment, and similarly, how the OEMs might regain the balance of power.

Finally, there is the question of luck. Why did Shimano so completely dominate the components sector in the 1980s? Was it simply because it was the only company to recognize the potential of the mountain bike, or the only one willing to invest in it? It might be argued that, because of its US market, the company was on the doorstep of the craze while its competitors were not, but this is not so: Suntour also had a presence in the USA. It is impossible to say how important it was to be in the right place at the right time, or how big a gamble the decision represented. What we can assert is that if firms do not take advantage of opportunities, they will not make any money out of them.

Strategy Models

There are a number of ways by which corporate strategy can be analyzed using different models and typologies. The following section considers a variety of models in the context of the Campagnolo/Shimano comparison.

Porter's Generic Strategy Model

The generic strategy model is appropriate because it starts with the assumption that the objective of all firms is survival rather than growth. This enables us to look at old and stable firms that return a healthy income to their shareholders, even if they have remained at a constant size. Campagnolo falls into this category (as do virtually all niche players). Campagnolo has taken a focused, differentiated approach, concentrating on the niche at the top end of the market (the serious cyclists), offering precision engineered, highly durable products. Shimano, on the other hand, differentiated on the basis of its speedy new product development and emphasis on environmental and leisure issues. However, while Porter suggests that successful firms choose to pursue either cost leadership or differentiation strategies, Shimano achieved both. Their heavy investment in R & D which led, among other things, to the cost advantages achieved from their cold forging technology is one example here. The company has also derived economies of scale and experience curve advantages from its market domination.

Leaders, Challengers, Followers and Nichers

Firms can also be classified according to whether they are market leaders, challengers, followers or nichers. Using this typology, Shimano is the market leader with about 76 per cent of the market (measured by derailleur sales); Suntour is a challenger with about 13 per cent of the market; Sachs-Huret is a follower with around eight per cent; and Mavic and Campagnolo are the nichers with two per cent and 0.5 per cent respectively.

Shimano is a classic market leader. It dominates the market in terms of sales, and sets the pace for competition, particularly in terms of new product introduction. In order to maintain its position, leaders must try to expand the total market and protect their market share. Shimano has expanded market size through its innovations and marketing, which convinced people that cycling is much more fun and easier than it once was. Also, by promoting mountain bikes, the company has helped to dramatically increase the size of the market. At the same time, Shimano has shrewdly defended its market share by investing heavily in R & D, introducing new products on a regular basis, and by plugging holes in the market, so that there is a Shimano product at every level. This has been particularly important as Shimano is selling to the OEMs, and needs to ensure that these customers have no reason to look elsewhere for supplies.

Challengers aim to erode the leader's market share by leapfrogging in some area where the leader has competitive advantage. So, for example, Suntour may attempt to be the first to the market with an innovation and thus take a technological initiative.

Followers like to keep up with the market by introducing their own versions of existing products developed elsewhere. While Sachs-Huret has tried to introduce products that others have not been interested in developing, it has been largely unsuccessful and it is still considered to be behind the Japanese.

Niche players try to serve segments that hold little interest to market leaders, thereby avoiding direct competition with them. They try to develop a deep understanding of customer needs, often by focusing on areas where there are complexities that demand levels of attention which larger firms are unable or unwilling to provide. With specialist knowledge, the niche player can command substantial margins if: the niche is large enough to be profitable; the niche has growth potential; the firm has the capabilities to serve the niche effectively; the firm is able to claim as part of its defensive armoury the goodwill of its customers; and the niche is of little interest to competitors. The first three are certainly true for the top end of the bicycle components sector, and the fourth is partially true for Campagnolo, in so far as professionals and top amateur competitors are generally loyal, even if other serious cyclists are turning to Shimano. The segment is of interest to others, however. Shimano is keen to make an impression and to gain the beneficial knock-on effects for serving the lower end customer segments. The niche is also a good environment for testing innovations.

Since there is always a risk of attack from a large competitor, or a chance that the niche itself will evaporate over time, it is usually advisable to operate in more than one niche. Campagnolo did so successfully in the 1960s and 1970s, by producing both sports racing products and precision instruments. When the company began to concentrate solely on bicycle components, it exposed itself to greater risk. On the other hand, if Campagnolo expands outside its niche, it may lose customers. Many people are attracted by the exclusivity of the Campagnolo brand. It would lose some of this appeal if virtually every bike on the shelf costing upwards of £100 were fitted with Campagnolo components. The message Campagnolo is projecting is 'not everyone can have a bike with Campagnolo components — you've got to know about bikes and be a serious cyclist.' There is less status attached to owning a Shimano bike.

Defenders, Prospectors, Analyzers and Reactors

According to this typology, Campagnolo most closely resembles the defender category, where the organization seeks to ensure stability by operating in a safe niche. These firms are not concerned with being at the technological sharp end of their industry, showing little interest in innovations that are not directly relevant to their own niche. Product range is narrow but is supposed to be of higher quality than that of competitors. These organizations prefer to grow by market penetration, if growth is an objective at all. Firms in this category sustain their products' positions through some kind of superiority (differentiation) with tight financial and administrative control to ensure that their position remains stable. There is some doubt about how financially prudent Campagnolo has been.

Shimano, on the other hand, would be classified as a prospector. These players are less risk-averse, willing to gamble with new products in the hope of extraordinary returns. First mover advantage is highly valued. These firms have wide product ranges, and regularly introduce and withdraw models. With Shimano, innovation and product management issues drive strategy, rather than bureaucracy. These firms display skills in marketing management and are likely to be more customer oriented than others, while defenders tend to be product orientated.

A hybrid of these two is the analyzer. Analyzers are less conservative than defenders when it comes to new product introduction, though they stick to a limited range that can comfortably be managed. The least successful strategy is that of the reactor which has no positive strategy, but responds to what the environment and competitors are doing. Neither Campagnolo nor Shimano fit into the analyzer or reactor categories.

Strategic Options

The following section examines some of the strategic options that are open to Campagnolo, and the costs and advantages associated with each.

Do Nothing or Withdraw

First, Campagnolo could decide to do nothing, though many analysts have pointed out that the adoption of this strategy usually means that the firm is not in touch with its environment, particularly in conditions of change. Withdrawing from the market is often seen as cowardly but can be a sensible move, particularly as it is preferable to a later forced withdrawal through insolvency. Neither of these options is appropriate for Campagnolo since the firm still has growth potential in the market.

Consolidation

This requires the firm to modify its way of operating, without changing its product range or the markets it operates in. In mature markets, a more defensive strategy is required using appropriate techniques; perhaps reducing costs, improving quality or increasing marketing expenditure. This option is of relevance to Campagnolo. It is faced with a situation of eroding market share and must seek ways by which to arrest the erosion.

Market Penetration

This suggests that firms may increase market share by improving their efficiency and thus reducing costs, or by improving their product quality, marketing or image, for example. This strategy would be more appropriate for Campagnolo later, assuming it can halt the decline.

Product Development

If Campagnolo were to invest resources into R & D, it might be able to gain the innovation initiative from Shimano. Many industry observers believe Campagnolo has the human resources and knowledge to do this, but it is questionable whether it has the financial resources needed to compete with Shimano at the moment. Campagnolo's product development strategies have been largely unsuccessful in the past, so one must question the chances of success. Many believe that Campagnolo does not possess the will to move into the mid-range sector. The company consists of perfectionists who are only interested in making products of ultimate quality. A move towards the lower end of the market would, however, give Campagnolo an opportunity to break into Shimano's dominant position with the OEMs.

Diversification

Although Campagnolo has operated in other markets in the past and has withdrawn, there may be a case for diversification. Shimano has successfully diversified in two ways: by entering into the fishing equipment sector by identifying commonalities in the technology (horizontal diversification); and by moving into the components servicing sector by introducing maintenance centres (forward integration). With its past experience and technical knowledge, it would not be difficult for Campagnolo to find related product areas. A successful diversification would reduce the company's current exposure in the bicycle components sector and possibly be the key to later withdrawal if necessary.

Postscript: What Actually Happened

In September 1992, just as this case was being written, Campagnolo announced the new Veloce groupset to the world. The groupset was clearly aimed at competing with Shimano's highly successful 105 mid-range group, which had been improved for 1993 by adding the dual control brake / gear lever option. The Veloce was to be offered with Campagnolo's dual control system, Ergopower, and was to retail at around £350, a price which was very competitive with the 105 price level. Many of the features were as advanced as those offered by Shimano and reviews suggested that the quality of the range was far superior to that of the previous Xenon group which comprised many low grade materials. Indeed, many items were considered to be of equal quality to those from the Athena and Chorus ranges, with some use of steel and resins instead of alloy. The products were well received by OEMs, many of whom exhibited the range on some of their new bikes at the Cologne Fair in October 1992. The company offered little new for its off-road ranges, though it is now believed that Campagnolo was catching up with Shimano in terms of technology.

Loblaws' G.R.E.E.N. Line

The theme of the class concerns whether Loblaws handled the development of the new line of green products appropriately. The line of 100 products, with 7 products endorsed by Pollution Probe, had been launched smoothly, but at a later press conference, Greenpeace attacked both Loblaws and Pollution Probe for marketing environmentally harmful products as 'green'. A similar attack from the Consumer Association followed shortly after. At about the same time, Colin Isaacs resigned as director of Pollution Probe, citing organizational tensions as the reason for his resignation.

The teaching objectives are: to introduce the concept of 'bridging organizations' and illustrate the need for business to be more sympathetic to the goals and fragile structures of these organizations if collaborative alliances are to be successful; to introduce students to marketing from a societal perspective; to facilitate an understanding of how product endorsements can best be used; and to understand reactions of social movement groups.

What motivated Loblaws to create a G.R.E.E.N. line and how successful was it from a marketing perspective and from a broader societal viewpoint?

In accordance with the marketing concept, Loblaws identified an unsatisfied consumer need in the Canadian marketplace and moved quickly to capitalize on it. Good management, according to the marketing concept, requires not only a focus on the customer, but also requires an organization which can respond effectively to changing customer needs. It holds long-run customer satisfaction to be the goal which must be achieved in order to ensure organizational success.

Given this business philosophy, Loblaws' G.R.E.E.N. line can be rated as successful but with one proviso. Loblaws certainly identified and focused on customer needs and wants, and responded in a timely fashion to changing customer needs; but where it can be criticized for falling short of the precepts of the marketing concept is in its implementation of the integrated marketing effort aimed at generating customer satisfaction. It is the product element of the marketing mix which was most problematic. In a rush to be the first to the market with a full line of green products, Loblaws included a number of products which even the average consumer might question, and which environmental movements such as Greenpeace openly attacked.

In addition, Loblaws appears to have compromised on product development. Only in the case of the organic fertilizer was Pollution Probe's expertise used for developmental purposes, and only this at Pollution Probe's initiative. In general, Loblaws appears to have dispensed with available scientific expertise and failed to utilize fully even the expertise of environmental groups, allying with them for purely promotional purposes. In the long run, this disregard may prove to have been short-sighted. If consumers conclude that Loblaws G.R.E.E.N. products are not truly green, Loblaws may have missed its strategic window, despite being the first to market. In some sense one is reminded of the American automobile manufacturers' attempts to meet consumer demand for smaller, more fuel-efficient cars. Detroit showed that it could do marketing research, identify consumer trends, and respond through advertising and promotion. Where it failed miserably was on product design: Detroit's product offerings were poorly thought out attempts to meet consumer needs and wants.

When the green products case is examined from a more macro perspective — the societal marketing concept — the initiative becomes even more problematic. Since the earliest days of the discipline, marketing scholars have been advocating a broadening of the marketing concept, away from the philosophy of pure and perfect competition, in the direction of acknowledging responsibility for the environment. On the other hand, it represents a philosophy much more akin to that of environmental groups and the emerging governmental definitions of sustainable development. The adoption of such a perspective on the part of business might well facilitate cooperative alliances with environmental groups. There is, however, no evidence that such concerns motivated the G.R.E.E.N. products initiative. The absence of product development, consultation, and careful product selection suggests that Loblaws was merely reacting to consumer demand. As a result, the alliance with Pollution Probe was not a satisfactory one.

Marketing has been criticized by writers arguing for a return to a greater role for R & D in product development, rather than a reliance on marketing research. These writers argue that strict adherence to the marketing concept has led to new products which are only cosmetically varied versions of existing products since consumers can only articulate wants that are close variants of existing products rather than revolutionary new ideas. Product innovation — not market research — is necessary to introduce radical new products to the market. This same argument is true for environmentally friendly products.

Writers have argued that business must lead the market with innovative green products. To do so, it must collaborate with those who have the expertise: the scientific community and the environmentalists. Moreover, it must treat those expert groups and individuals who are willing to collaborate as a valuable resource, and gain some understanding of the strong values and sometimes fragile structures which underlie such groups.

What motivated Pollution Probe and Greenpeace? Could Loblaws have predicted the reactions of these groups to product endorsement?

Cited among the consequences of Loblaws' pursuit of endorsements is the rift that occurred in the previously cooperative environmental movement industry. An application of resource mobilization theory is helpful in understanding the dynamics underlying the responses of both Pollution Probe and Greenpeace. Using this perspective, social movements are viewed as actors in a field populated by other similar social movements, and in competition for resources with them. These resources include labour, money, use of the media, and access to institutional structures.

From the beginning, Greenpeace has projected the image of passive resistance. What they packaged was not only environmental protection, but heroic adventure. This kind of organizational charisma was unique among the environmental movements in Canada, and hence represented a competitive advantage. This strategy made it crucial that Greenpeace avoid engaging the institutional structures of business or government in mobilizing resources. Conversely, it was equally crucial that they have access to the media, who alone could capture and broadcast the heroic images which 'sold' them to supporters. Greenpeace was able to use the media extremely effectively to mobilize resources. As its ideology dictated that, for the most part, Greenpeace appeals to individuals and not to other organizations, mass media was important in order to reach as wide an audience as possible. Although Greenpeace also runs door-to-door and direct mail campaigns, it is still the media that keeps alive in the public's mind the heroic element which is an essential part of the Greenpeace product.

Pollution Probe, on the other hand, has had a much lower profile from the beginning. It was founded in a university setting and has been associated with the development of environmental studies programmes. Among the programmes and services it offers are: executing and publishing studies on pollution, acid rain, food additives, radiation, and recycling strategies; sending out speakers and conducting workshops for teachers and students; running the Economy Store in Toronto; and publishing a quarterly newspaper (*Probe Post*) which is sent to members. For support, Pollution Probe has always depended on small grants from businesses, government contracts, and individual donors. These structures cannot provide the kind of access to the wider public that Greenpeace has mobilized. Pollution Probe's product has never been easy to 'package' or 'market'. It is essentially an organization for collecting and processing information, and therefore its appeal to wide segments of the general population has been hard to define.

From this vantage point it is easy to understand Isaacs' interest in Loblaws' product endorsements. By associating with Loblaws, Pollution Probe gained instant access to a huge group of consumers. Pollution Probe's name would be on the packages of the endorsed products, so it would be associated with tangible products which would be marketed by the Loblaws marketing machinery. In other words, the product endorsements gave Pollution Probe superb access to a powerful institutional structure with which to publicize itself.

It was not surprising that such a strategy provoked attacks from other environmental groups. Even in cooperative fields, when one social movement organization gains access to institutional structures which are not available to other such organizations, conflict is likely to erupt. Where other organizations are competing for similar audiences, conflict is apt to become more rancorous. It is not likely that individual constituents will support both organizations.

From this viewpoint, two separate but related aspects of Greenpeace's response become apparent. First, it is likely that some of the rancour was purely competitive: Pollution Probe had now gained access, through Loblaws' advertising, to a mass of 'consumers' who, while never willing to become activists themselves, were willing to support others in these activities. Loblaws' advertising campaign encouraged these people to feel that 'you can make a difference', that they too could become 'activists' simply by buying the product. Were consumers to buy this message, as well as the product, would their interest in living vicariously through Greenpeace diminish? By allying with Loblaws, Pollution Probe directly attacked Greenpeace's competitive advantage — its appeal to the mass of well-intentioned, affluent but passive supporters.

On another level, Greenpeace was able to turn the threat into an opportunity, both for media attention and to further differentiate its 'product'. By calling a press conference, Greenpeace was on familiar ground, and mobilizing familiar resources. It effectively used the media to, first, stage a drama — the potential toxicity of a product labelled 'green' — and, then, to set the agenda for how consumers should think about green products in general. Thus, the particular position adopted by Greenpeace helped to reaffirm and to reassert the movement as pure, uncompromising, committed, and fearless.

For Pollution Probe, however, the issue was more complex. The strategy of resource mobilization backfired, causing severe tensions and splits in the organization. From a micro perspective, the splits that divided Pollution Probe may be viewed as an effect of poor management.   Despite the new organizational structure which placed decision-making authority in the hands of the executive committee, Isaacs should have realized that the haste and secrecy with which he attempted to close the deal with Loblaws violated the ethics of consensus decision-making valued by many of the staff.

Viewed from a wider perspective of the environmental movement as a whole, however, the disorganization of Pollution Probe takes on a different light: as one of the central threats confronting any organization attempting to play an intersectoral 'bridging' role in the interests of larger societal goals.

Pollution Probe tried to play an intersectoral 'bridging' role between the business and environmental industries. Were they successful? Why not?

Despite their potential strategic importance, bridging organizations are beset with potential problems. They must essentially find mechanisms to provide integration of organizations which may be wildly disparate in terms of wealth, power, culture, language, values, interest, and structural characteristics. The farther apart these organizations are and the more focused the objective of the specific operations, the more difficult the problem becomes. As long as the bridging organization can continue to integrate these perspectives internally, it can continue to function as a bridge for other external organizations. But if, for a variety of circumstances, the different viewpoints become points of factional contention within the bridging organization itself, the organization is severely weakened in its external bridging capacity.

Loblaws differs from most environmental groups in its definition of time span for action, ultimate goals, processes of decision-making and patterns of communication.   The objective in this case was extremely focused (the endorsement of seven products which Loblaws was to name), which reduced the ability of the two organizations to retain their goal autonomy. As a result, the pressures produced internal stress lines in Pollution Probe.

In addition, the two chief process issues which were identified by Pollution Probe staff, the issues of timing and secrecy, were in fact imposed by Loblaws' desire to be first to market. Had Loblaws been prepared to try to understand Pollution Probe to the same extent that Isaacs was prepared to understand the imperatives motivating Loblaws' rush to market, the case might have ended differently.

Conglom Inc

The Conglom case shows a range of ways in which control can be exerted — from a reliance on instrumental power to the use of symbolic, unobtrusive power through the complex conference process. It also illustrates how middle managers at ELB were involved in strategy making through the conference, creating a collective vision or strategy for the company.

As far as Conglom was concerned, as in the case of all conglomerates that acquire a diverse range of operating companies, there is an inherent tension between corporate headquarters and the unit companies. The former wants to exercise some control but the latter has most of the knowledge and expertise. Conglomerates typically adopt one of three approaches in managing their operating companies or divisions: strategic planning, where the corporate centre undertakes the duties of strategic decision making both in terms of the overall composition of the portfolio and the long-term direction of individual businesses; financial control, where the centre refuses to take strategic responsibility but sets and monitors clear financial objectives within which units have to realize their own strategic objectives; and strategic control, where the centre tries to control units through both financial and strategic objectives.

There are disadvantages with each of these three approaches. Strategic planning immerses corporate management in the formulation of long-term objectives that are difficult to enforce in the form of short-term financial controls. Unit management may resist the interference of distant corporate managers whose knowledge of their business is sketchy and outdated. Financial controls allow unambiguous targets to be set but the danger is that long-term strategic goals will be sacrificed for short-term financial objectives. The strategic control approach tries to avoid the shortcomings of the other two by focusing both strategically and financially on core businesses. In reality, however, it often combines the disadvantages of the two other approaches because strategic measures are inevitably more vague and do not sit well with financial measures, while unit management continues to resent the interference.

All material and quotations taken from: J. Roberts, "Strategy and Accounting in a UK Conglomerate", *Accounting, Organizations and Society*, 12 (1/2), 107-26, 1990.

Conglom's philosophy was one of focusing on financial controls and distancing itself from its operations. The challenge was: how to allow unit managers autonomy and, at the same time, ensure that they continued to work towards Conglom's goals. A number of mechanisms were used to align the self-interest of unit managers with corporate objectives: financial controls tracked performance; possible dismissal or divestment represented a threat; bonuses, stock options and career opportunities acted as positive incentives; and finance directors were socialized at and linked to corporate headquarters.

Conglom's approach represented an acknowledgement of the limits of its knowledge and expertise, and a commitment to performance rather than to people. As far as the former was concerned, Conglom's actions forged a mixed message: while ELB managers supposedly had the freedom to take strategic responsibility for their business, Conglom's decision to divest all its overseas operations sharply limited that strategic manoeuvrability. The latter served to alienate ELB managers as their objections were ignored and their participation in setting financial targets limited.

Bill Thornton effectively duplicated some of Conglom's controls, notably the use of performance measures backed up by a threat of adverse consequences in the event of unsatisfactory performance. In this case, he continued to rely on instrumental sources of power. It was backed up, however, by his use of unobtrusive power through the conference process. This iterative, cumulative process was both a calculated technique and a social process into which the 'controllers' were drawn as all members of the ELB became committed to the overarching, collective strategy.

Conglom Inc (B)

Thornton organized an annual conference where senior ELB managers reported to middle management (from both ELB's Head Office and the factories) on the past year's activity and the plans for the coming year. It was a time consuming and intensive activity that, nonetheless, had considerable benefits. Each year, the conference was preceded with a tour by Thornton of the factories, followed by a two-day pre-conference meeting of the top twenty or so managers when they reviewed the past year and formulated plans for the coming year. Having agreed on the outline for the main conference, the managers returned to their jobs and began to work on their individual presentations with their subordinates. A three-day rehearsal preceded the conference itself. These meetings helped to form an integrated, collective picture of ELB.

> Well, I think it's rudimentary really. You give them the facts of the business honestly. It was obvious to them that the whole of the senior team had worked very hard preparing an in-depth analysis of the business. It wasn't just me, it was all my colleagues, it was a number of the factory managers, it was managers of the trading division. Collectively, it added up to a very powerful story. . . . I think the main thing that came through was that it was all true basically. People seem somehow to prefer to know the truth even if it's bad news than to be kidded along. (Bill Thornton)

The factory tour provided an opportunity for a series of face-to-face conversations which set the tone for relatively open communication. While strategy formulation remained the responsibility of divisional management, such conversations informed Thornton and his senior managers and improved their understanding. The pre-conference meeting provided a context in which senior managers could inform and be informed about what was happening in the company as a whole, and where partial insights could be integrated into a coherent picture which enabled everyone to locate the significance of their own actions. On this basis, collective responses were gradually built up allowing individual plans to be formulated in the context of the whole. The individual presentations of managers brought in another group of subordinates, thus widening the collective process further. The preparation for and staging of the conference itself forced those managers making presentations to clarify their thinking. During the rehearsal, an integrated, collective picture of ELB was finally developed.

The conference meeting itself built on the shared understanding and knowledge as well as a complex system of reciprocal rights and obligations. It created a credible picture of external reality and generated strong mutual commitment. It was this collective view rather than the will and formal authority of the CEO that dictated action. Whilst it is often possible and plausible to resist the will of an individual, it makes no sense to try and avoid a more pervasive reality. The collective picture released senior managers from the necessity of using their formal powers coercively or, at the very least, legitimated coercion in the event of obvious 'dissidents'.

The conference meetings also reduced the likelihood of 'bad' decisions by opening up the decision making process.

> Basically, there's a high risk strategy with this kind of approach, because if you've got the wrong solution, that group of people in the audience, individually and collectively, knows everything about the business. So if what you are putting forward is a stupid strategy your power evaporates. It won't necessarily be obvious that it has evaporated, but it has. From then on you're basically powerless in the business and so it's only a matter of time before you get found out and turfed out. (Bill Thornton)

Collectively, senior management had to submit their thinking and actions to the scrutiny of their subordinates — if their story was incredible, contradictory or inconsistent, it would be obvious.

> If some of the assumptions are wrong or the solutions impracticable, the credibility vanishes, you move into a kind of passive resistance zone. You can't do anything, you've lost the means to make decisions possible. If you try to do it by bribing or promoting, you can (only) do a certain amount. (Manager)

The conference meetings sometimes led to different functional areas blaming and challenging each other. But, by providing a context where conflicts could surface *and* be managed constructively, the conference drew individuals into making reciprocal commitments which were advertised to middle management at the main conference.

> The senior management were demonstrating commitment to the middle management and they're demonstrating the team thing as well and everything feeds in together. What each guy says is supportive of what the others are saying. So all the elements are there and all the senior guys are committing themselves, so actually this commitment thing becomes a normal behaviour and the teamwork thing becomes a normal behaviour and so suddenly you've got a quite different climate in the company. (Manager)

So, although the collective presentation of the picture was often difficult, it was vital to ensure that when people were asked to take difficult decisions, they had some understanding of why they were necessary. Moreover, the public commitments countered the potentially centrifugal forces of decentralization. So, even when the meetings raised conflicts, they also produced a series of agreements, 'deals', and 'contracts' between managers in different functions and factories. In this way, managers were forced to work cooperatively.

In conclusion, the conference process enabled managers to deal with constantly falling numbers; reflecting the decline in sales volume. The number of employees fell from 6,000 to 1,600 with little or no resistance from managers. During the first six years of Thornton's tenure, ELB return on capital employed rose from 12 per cent to over 100 per cent; profits doubled from £18 million to £37 million on reduced sales.

In December 1983, Conglom launched another hostile bid for a UK company which responded with an attack on Conglom's track record. The threatened company took out full-page advertisements with a broken light bulb on them which argued that the real cost of the ELB takeover had been layoffs, high prices and low investment: the 'hands off' policy was really a 'sell off' policy. For the first time, some of the private concerns of ELB managers were being publicly articulated by outsiders. About this time, ELB managers made a proposal to corporate management for an investment of several million pounds to improve machine productivity. The payback on the investment exceeded Conglom's usual rules and would cause something of a dip in Return on Capital Employed. Conglom made an improved offer and was successful in its takeover bid. Shortly afterwards, ELB management received corporate approval for their capital expenditure plans.

Questions

- Why do you think Bill Thornton was successful?
- What benefits were derived from the conference?
- What sources of power underlay Thornton's actions?